GOD
&
HUMAN BEINGS

FIRST ENGLISH TRANSLATION

GOD & HUMAN BEINGS

Voltaire

Translated by Michael Shreve

Introduction by S. T. Joshi

 Prometheus Books

59 John Glenn Drive
Amherst, New York 14228–2119

Published 2010 by Prometheus Books

Inquiries should be addressed to
Prometheus Books
59 John Glenn Drive
Amherst, New York 14228–2119
VOICE: 716–691–0133
FAX: 716–691–0137
WWW.PROMETHEUSBOOKS.COM

14 13 12 11 10   5 4 3 2

Library of Congress Cataloging-in-Publication Data

Voltaire, 1694–1778.
    [Dieu et les hommes. English]
    God and human beings : / by Voltaire ; first English translation, by Michael Shreve.
        p. cm.
    Includes bibliographical references and index.
    ISBN 978–1–61614–178–3 (pbk. : alk. paper)
    1. Christianity—Controversial literature. 2. Judaism—Controversial literature. 3. Bible—Controversial literature. 4. Religion. I. Shreve, Mike. II. Title.

BL2776.V613 2010
200.9—dc22

                                                          2010004025

Printed in the United States of America on acid-free paper

Contents

Translator's Note on the Text

God and Human Beings was first published in 1769. It was said to be written by Dr. Obern, who was completely fictitious, and translated from the English by Jacques Aimon. Now, this name may refer to a friend of Voltaire's youth who died in 1731 or to Jean Aymon, the domestic prelate of Pope Alexander XI who became an apostate and relapsed heretic after having stolen some manuscripts from the Bibliothèque du Roi (The King's Library, which became the Bibliothèque Nationale).

But, whether it was because Voltaire was an author of "good standing" and wanted to represent the philosophy of the lower classes or because the work was scandalous and he wanted to escape the censors, or to align himself with English religious tolerance, in any case it was not at all uncommon at that time to write under a pseudonym. (We can recall that *Candide* was "translated from the German of Docteur Ralph" in 1759.) But this is Voltaire. In fact, it is basically drawn from *Questions sur l'Encyclopédie* (published between 1770–1772), the longest of any of his works.

On its publication critics called *God and Human Beings* the work of the devil promoting atheism. It was condemned to be burned along with a number of d'Holbach's works by the Parlement de Paris on August 18, 1770 because it was considered a sarcastic and bitter treatise hostile to the Christian religion, which it treated as the most contemptible and foolish production of the human species. Voltaire is surely guilty of the accusation of anti-Church, anti-Catholic sentiments, but he is far from being an atheist (see chapter 36, where he makes the atheist priest Jean Meslier pray to God on his deathbed—an invention of Voltaire). In fact, this is one of the works in which he combats atheism in support of his deism, and his readers should always keep this in mind: Yes, we want a religion, but a simple one, wise, august, less unworthy of God and made more for us; in a word, we want to serve "God and human beings" (chapter 44).

The present translation is based on the text established by R. Mortier, *The Complete Works of Voltaire*, volume 69, Oxford, The Voltaire Foundation, 1994. Citations are translated from the text of Voltaire even where they differ from the original. References are given in brackets where they are lacking in the text.

Introduction

S. T. Joshi

François Marie Arouet (1694–1778), who adopted the pseudonym Voltaire early in his career, gained such celebrity, both during and after his lifetime, as a critic of religion that it is understandable why many would wish to see him as an outright atheist and freethinker. But, as the following work—translated into English for the first time since its publication in 1769—clearly indicates, Voltaire was anything but an atheist, although his searing anticlericalism, his disdain for "miracles" and theological disputation, and in particular his deep loathing of the cruelties practiced in religion's name all contributed to the evolution of a viable atheist viewpoint.

Voltaire's personal history, as well as the political and social history of Europe during his time, contributed directly to the fervency of his anticlericalism. His early education at a school called Louis-le-Grand, where he came into contact with freethinkers, such as the young Denis Diderot and Claude Adrien Helvétius, led him to write a verse satire, "Le Vrai Dieu" (1715; "The True God"), mocking the notion of a god killing himself for the sake of sinners. This satirical tendency manifested itself in a great many subsequent works—plays, novels, and even sober works of history and philosophy—of which the most notable are *La Pucelle* (1755; usually translated as *The Maid of Orleans*), in which the hapless Joan of Arc perpetually fends off attacks on her virginity, and the imperishable *Candide* (1759), which, in its demolition of Leibniz's argument that this is the "best of all possible worlds," seriously called into question the notion of an omnipotent and benevolent god.

For these and other works, Voltaire became an exile from his own country. He had already been forced to leave France in the years 1726–1729 because he had offended a nobleman who easily could have had him thrown into prison. Voltaire went to England, where he was struck with what he perceived to be both the religious toleration enshrined in the English constitution and the lively and vigorous antireligious thinking enunciated by such philosophers as Lord Bolingbroke and others. Voltaire was also affected by the science of Sir Isaac Newton, which established the universe as operating under fixed laws, and the philosophy of John Locke, whose sane empiricism put to shame the abstract Cartesianism of Descartes and others. It is, therefore, no accident that, when decades later Voltaire came to write *God and Human Beings* (Dieu et les hommes), he chose to pretend that it was written by an Englishman.

The impassioned nature of this work and others in Voltaire's output is a direct result of the political, intellectual, and social repression of absolutist France of his time. Voltaire did, of course, suffer personally under Louis XV and Louis XVI, but he saw his own persecution as symptomatic of the evils of the union of religion and politics in a monarch who was little better than a dictator. His *Lettres philosophiques* (1734; a translation of the work he had written in English as *Letters concerning the English Nation*, 1733) was publicly burned; Louis XV, offended that Voltaire would desert France to spend time with his hated rival, Frederick the Great of Prussia, during the period 1750–1755, forbade him to reenter France; and *La Pucelle*, pungently satirizing one of the icons of French history, did not help Voltaire in returning to the king's good graces. By 1758 Voltaire, after a few years spent in Geneva, had chosen to settle in Ferney, on the French side of the border between France and Switzerland. It was sufficiently far from Paris that he need not fear persecution by the king, but sufficiently close that French intellectuals—and, indeed, writers and thinkers throughout Europe—could make pilgrimages there to pay homage to one of the word's most influential philosophers.

God and Human Beings was the culminating work of a decade

that saw some of Voltaire's most celebrated philosophical works: the *Dictionnaire philosophique* (1764; *Philosophical Dictionary*); the *Philosophe de l'histoire* (1765; *The Philosophy of History*); *Questions sur les miracles* (1767; *Questions on Miracles*); and *Examen important de milord Bolingbroke* (1767; *Lord Bolingbroke's Important Examination*), itself a work purportedly written by Bolingbroke and another ferocious attack on Christian theology. It is no accident that *God and Human Beings* was condemned as the work of an impious atheist.

But, in fact, Voltaire was not an atheist, but a deist. It would seem that he could not conceive how the universe came into being without a creator. Even Newton, who established the laws of nature, accepted the deist metaphor of God as a clockmaker who began the mechanism and then (rather like the gods as envisioned by Epicurus, who exist in the spaces between the stars but have no involvement in human affairs) let the universe operate of its own accord. It is not surprising that Voltaire was stumped by the argument from design; as he wrote in the entry "God, Gods" in the *Philosophical Dictionary*: "Every construction which displays means and an end announces an artisan; therefore this universe, composed of mechanisms, of means, each of which has its end, reveals a very powerful, very intelligent creator." The atheists of the day did not really have a satisfactory explanation of this problem themselves, and it required Darwin's theory of evolution to overthrow the argument from design, at least as far as the development of life on this planet was concerned.

Voltaire was also concerned about the basis of morality. Indeed, he saw (true) religion as essentially concerned with morality; as he writes in *God and Human Beings*: "Religion surely consists in virtue and not in the impertinent frivolities of theology." Well and good; but why can't virtue be self-generated, rather than dependent on a god? In this treatise Voltaire merely states, "Morality comes from God; it is uniform everywhere." Atheists would dispute both halves of that utterance; indeed, the widely varying moralities practiced by different cultures and different religions is one of the chief anthropological arguments that atheists have brought against the notion of a god who dictates morality to human beings. In *God and Human Beings* Voltaire does not elaborate on this point, but in other works he does. A dialogue titled "The Sage and the Atheist" displays a "sage" convincing an atheist with surprising ease that the existence of a conscience proves the existence of a god who is the source of all morality ("God, in thus speaking to your heart, has commanded you to abstain from crime"). It is for this reason that, in *God and Human Beings* and elsewhere, Voltaire systematically criticizes atheists as threats to morality and, hence, social cohesion.

In spite of the questionable deist assumptions Voltaire made throughout his career, *God and Human Beings* is nonetheless a vibrant and pioneering work. It is nothing less than an exercise in comparative religion—indeed, a compressed history of the Christian religion extending back to its Jewish roots and beyond. Voltaire had already broached this issue in *The Philosophy of History*, but he substantially expands upon it here. When, in speaking of Jewish history, Voltaire declares, "I will examine this history like the history of Livy or Herodotus," he is anticipating the "higher criticism" of the nineteenth century regarding the Scriptures (both the Old and the New Testaments) as historical works subject to critical scrutiny just like any other ancient work that has come down to us; the superstitious reverence with which the Bible was held by its partisans—a reverence that censured as blasphemous any analysis even of its purported statements of fact, let alone its dogmatic assertions about the existence and nature of deity—was something Voltaire, as a philosopher of history, could not countenance. In his frank and at times satirical discussion of Jewish history, Voltaire not merely denies that the Pentateuch was written by Moses but doubts the very existence of Moses. He keenly draws upon the history of other ancient nations—the Greeks, the Indians, the Assyrians—to show that much of the "history" of the ancient Israelites might have been borrowed from the history or legends of other lands.

When it comes to Jesus, however, Voltaire adopts a tone of studied respect. It is plain that he has considerable admiration for the person and the morals of Jesus himself—at least as he understood them. Although he is forthright in stating that the story of Jesus must also be scrutinized like any other historical account, he resists the temptation—already evident among freethinkers of the period—to doubt Jesus' very existence. While acknowledging the manifest errors and contradictions in the Gospels regarding certain phases of Jesus' life, and while noting that Jesus is not even mentioned in contemporaneous texts by other nations (especially the Romans), the farthest that Voltaire will go is to say that Jesus did indeed exist but was merely "hidden": he was such an obscure figure that the Romans and others simply did not take notice of him.

It is not entirely clear why Voltaire is so intent on absolving Jesus of the subsequent horrors of Christianity, to the point of declaring pungently that "Jesus was not a Christian." Voltaire wants to see Jesus as an example and forerunner of the kind of religious toleration that he saw in England and that he strove to make universal. At the same time, Voltaire is clear on the notion that Jesus was in no way a divine figure: he shrewdly notes that it is only in the Gospel of John that Jesus' divinity is put forward, and elsewhere he points out that many of the more absurd and paradoxical features of Christian theology—such as the doctrine of the Trinity, which Voltaire cannot lampoon frequently enough—very likely came from Neoplatonism.

Voltaire reserves his most vitriolic attacks for the long and bloody history of the Christian church, especially during those centuries when it controlled the reins of government throughout Europe. The remarkable chapter 42 of *God and Human Beings*, in which Voltaire presents a very conservative summary of the number of human beings—mostly purported "heretics"—who have been killed by the church is a tour de force of bland satire. The total number—nearly 10 million—is, as Voltaire plainly states, probably a low-ball figure (and it is not clear that he has counted the hundreds of thousands of suspected "witches" killed in both the Catholic and Protestant countries, unless some of these are included in the 200,000 that he declares were executed by the Inquisition). This issue—the ability of a church to enforce its dogmas by the use of secular power—was perhaps the one that fired Voltaire's righteous indignation more than any other. Let us recall that it was earlier in the decade of the 1760s that the celebrated case of Jean Calas—the Protestant who, accused of murdering his son because the latter had converted to Roman Catholicism, was tortured and put to death by the state—led to the writing of the *Traité sur la tolérance* (1763; *Treatise on Toleration*), in which Voltaire's plea for religious toleration and freedom of thought found its most impassioned expression.

What Voltaire sought to do, both in *God and Human Beings* and in his other writings, was to present a religion shorn of dogma and doctrinal disputation over meaningless and insignificant issues, and especially a religion that refused to suppress free inquiry and persecute its opponents. The kind of religion Voltaire advocates at the end of this treatise—"simple, august, less unworthy of God and made more for us"—is perhaps not far from the agnosticism that many people practice today. If Voltaire could have overcome his prejudice against atheists as a band of libertines who practiced no morals at all because they refused to fear postmortem punishment, then he might have fallen into the atheist camp himself. As it is, Voltaire's searching criticism of Christianity—both on the basis of its flawed dogmas and, especially, on the basis of its pernicious misuse of secular authority for centuries—remains as vital and as timely as ever, and serves as an eternally relevant warning that the battle against religious oppression must never be abandoned.

Chapter 1

Our Crimes and Stupidities

In general men are stupid, ungrateful, jealous, greedy for other people's goods, abusive of their superiority when strong, and deceitful when weak.

Women, born with more delicate and less hardy organs than men, are normally more cunning and less barbaric. This is so true that among a thousand criminals who are put to death, you will hardly find three or four women. It is also true that you will encounter some hardy women as cruel as men, but this is very rare.

Power is usually in the hands of men in the state and families only because they have a stronger fist, a steadier mind, and a harder heart. From all this, moralists of every age have concluded that the human species is not worth much, and in this they are not very far from the truth.

It's not that men are irresistibly carried away by their nature to do the evil they always do. If this fatal opinion were true, the earth would have lost its inhabitants a long time ago. It is a contradiction in terms to say that the human race is compelled to destroy itself and yet continues to exist.

I believe that of a hundred young women with old husbands, there are at least ninety-nine who sincerely want them dead, but you will hardly find one who wants to take it upon herself to poison the man for whom she would like to veil herself in black. Patricides and fratricides are common nowhere. What, then, is the extent and limit of our crimes? It is the degree of violence in our passions, the degree of our power and reason.

We have intermittent fevers, continual fevers that get worse and delirium, but very rarely rage. There are people who are healthy. Our intermittent fevers are the wars with neighboring people. Our delirium is the murder that anger or vengeance incites us to commit against our fellow citizens. When we murder our loved ones or make them unhappier than if we had killed them, when the fanatic hypocrites light the fires of the stake, that is rage. I will not go into detail here about other sicknesses, that is to say, lesser, innumerable crimes that afflict society.

Why have we waged war for so long and why have we committed this crime without any remorse? We wage war solely to harvest the wheat that others have sown, to take their sheep, horses, cattle, and furniture. That is to what everything is reduced because that is the sole principle of all riches. It is ridiculous to think that Romulus celebrated games in a miserable little village between three bare mountains and that he invited to these games three hundred girls from the area to snatch them away. But it is certain enough that he and his partners took the animals and plows of the Sabines.

Charlemagne waged war for thirty years on the poor Saxons for a tribute of five hundred cows. I don't deny that during the course of these thefts, Romulus and his senators, Charlemagne and his dozen peers raped many girls, and perhaps by mutual consent, but it is clear that the real objective of war was to have the cows, hay, and so on— in a word, to steal.

Even today a hero has a half guinea a day to enter with the subordinate heroes and their four or five sous into the country of another august sovereign in the name of his august master and start ordering all the farmers to supply cattle, sheep, hay, straw, wheat, wine, wood, linens, blankets, and the like. I read the other day in a little chronological history of our neighbor France, written by a magistrate, these remarkable words: "Great forage on the 11th of October 1709 where the Count of Broglie defeated the Prince of Lobkowitz," that is, on the tenth of October he killed five or six hundred Germans who were defending their hay. Afterward the French, already defeated at Malplaquet, lost the city of Mons. Well, this forage was without a doubt an exploit worthy of eternal remembrance! But this destitution shows us that basically in all the wars from Troy until today it's only been about stealing.

This is so unfortunately true that the name of thief and soldier were once synonymous in all nations. Look at the *Miles* of Plautus: "*latrocinatus annos decem mercedem accipio*" ("I was a thief for ten years and got paid"). "King Seleucus commissioned me to muster thieves for him" [2 Macc. 3:7]. See the Old Testament: "Jephthah, son of Gilead and a prostitute hired brigands" [Judg. 1:11]; "Abimelech mustered a gang of brigands" [Judg. 9:4]; "David gathered four hundred desperately lawless thieves" [1 Sam. 22:2]; and so on.

When the chief of the Malandrins, the brigands, had killed and stolen enough, he enslaved the hapless victims who were still alive. They became serfs or subjects, which in nine-tenths of the earth is pretty much the same thing. Genseric usurped the title of king. He soon became a sacred man and took our goods, our women, and our lives, by divine right, if we let him.

Add to all these public thefts the innumerable secret thefts that have ruined families, the calumnies, the ingratitude, the insolence of the strong and the deceit of the weak, and you will conclude that the human race has almost never lived except in misfortune and in fear worse than misfortune itself.

I said that all the horrors that follow upon war were committed without the least remorse. Nothing is truer. No one is ashamed of what they do in a group. Each is encouraged by the example of others; he who massacres and pillages the most has the glory. A soldier, when taking Bergen-op-Zoom, cried out, "I'm bored of killing, I'm going to rape," and everyone clapped their hands.

Remorse, on the other hand, is for him who, not heartened by his companions, limits himself to killing and stealing in secret. He is horrified by it until habit hardens him as much as the others who abandon themselves to crime on a regular basis and on the front lines.

Chapter 2

Remedy Approved by the Body of Doctors against the Above Sicknesses

The nations that are called civilized because they are mean and vicious in cities instead of in the country or caves find no more powerful antidote against what devours most hearts than recourse to God, the rewarder and revenger.

Though city magistrates made laws against theft and adultery, they themselves were robbed in their homes while they were promulgating their laws in public; and their wives took this time to mock them with their lovers.

So, what other restraint could they put on cupidity, on secret, unpunished transgressions than the idea of an eternal master who sees us and will judge us even in our innermost thoughts? We don't know who first taught this doctrine to men. If I knew and was sure that he didn't go too far, that he didn't corrupt the medicine he was offering to men, I would put him on an altar.

Hobbes says that he would have him hanged. His reason, he says, is that this apostle of God stands up against the public power, which he calls Leviathan, by coming to offer men a higher master than Leviathan, than the legislative sovereignty.

The sentence of Hobbes seems very hard to me. I agree with him that this apostle would be very punishable if he came to say to our parliament or to the king of Spain or to the Senate in Venice, "I come to proclaim to you a God whose minister I am; he gave me the responsibility of imprisoning you to my will, of taking away your goods, of killing you if you do the slightest thing to displease me. I will murder you like the holy man Ehud murdered Eglon king of Moab and the Jews [Judg. 3:20], like the priest Jehoiada murdered Athaliah at the horses' entrance [2 Kings 11:16] and like wise Solomon murdered his brother Adonijah [1Kings 2:25]," and so forth.

I admit that if a preacher came to speak to us like this, either in the Upper or Lower House or in the Drawing Room, I would vote to strangle the rascal.

But if the atheists ruled among us, as is said happened in London in the time of Charles II and at Rome in the times of Sixtus IV, Alexander VI, Leon X, and so on, I would be very grateful to an honest man, like Plato or Marcus Aurelius or Epictetus, to come and simply tell us, "Mortals, there is a just God, be just." I see no reason at all to hang such a citizen.

Although I claim to be very tolerant, I am inclined to punish whoever would say today, "Ladies and Gentlemen, there is no God. Slander, betray, deceive, steal, murder, poison, it's all the same as long as you are the strongest and most clever." It is clear that this man would be very pernicious to society, no matter what the Reverend Father Malagrida says—the former Jesuit, who, they say, persuaded an entire family that it was not a venial sin to assassinate the king of Portugal in a particular case.

Chapter 3

A God among All Civilized Nations

When a nation is assembled into a society, it needs the worship of a God in proportion as the citizens need to help one another. That's why there has never been a nation assembled under laws that hasn't recognized a divinity since time immemorial.

Did the Supreme Being reveal itself to those who first said that it was necessary to love and fear a God who punished crime and rewarded virtue? Undoubtedly not. God didn't speak to Thoth, the Egyptian lawmaker, to Brahma of the Indians, to Orpheus of Thrace, to Zoroaster of the Persians, and so forth.

But, he is found in all nations of men who had enough common sense to teach this useful doctrine, just like there were men who taught arithmetic, geometry, and astronomy by force of their reason.

By measuring the fields, one found that the triangle is half of a square and that triangles with the same base and height are equal. Another, by sowing and reaping and guarding his sheep, noticed that the sun and moon returned to nearly the same point that the stars had left and that they didn't go beyond a certain northern and southern limit. A third thought that human beings, animals, and stars did not make themselves and saw that a Supreme Being existed. A fourth, alarmed at the wrongs that men did to one another, concluded that there was a Being who made the stars, earth, and human beings, and this Being should reward honest men and punish the wicked. This idea is so natural and honest that it was easily accepted.

The same force of our understanding that made us know arithmetic, geometry, and astronomy and made us invent laws also made us know God. It takes only two or three good arguments, such as we see in Plato, among many bad ones to worship the Divinity. You don't need a revelation to know that the sun corresponds to different stars from one month to another. You don't need a revelation to understand that human beings did not make themselves and that we depend on a higher Being of some sort.

But, if some charlatans tell me that there is a power in numbers, if by measuring my fields they deceive me, if by observing the stars they claim that this star controls my destiny, if by telling me about a just god they order me to give my goods to them for this god, then I will call them all rogues and try to conduct myself alone with what little reason God has given me.

Chapter 4

On Ancient Worship and Firstly in China

The older a nation is, the older its religion is, too.

Today when there are no longer Jesuits to flatter or hate in most of Europe, when there is no longer any value in fighting their most reasonable, as well as their most ridiculous, opinions and the hate they well deserved has been snuffed out with them, it must be agreed that they were right when they affirmed that the Chinese government had never been atheist. This impertinent paradox was promoted in Europe because the Jesuits had become very prestigious in China before they were chased out. In Paris they wanted them to promote their atheism in Peking because they were persecutors in Paris.

It is with this same sectarian spirit, with the folly connected to all pedantic arguments, that the Sorbonne dared to condemn at the same time both Bayle, who maintained that a society of atheists could survive, and the Jesuits, whom they accused of supporting the atheist government of the Chinese, so that these ridiculous pedagogues of the Sorbonne pronounced the for and against at the same time, the yes and the no, which almost always happens to them and their kind. They said to Bayle, "It is impossible for there to be a group of atheists in the world," and to the Jesuits, "The court in Peking is atheist and so are you." And the Jesuit Hardouin answered them, "Yes, there are groups of atheists because you are them, Arnaud, Pascal, Quesnel, and Petit-pied." This priestly madness has been dealt with in many good books, but we must find out here the pretext that seemed to color the reproach of atheism that our Western scholars made of the most respectable nation of the East. The ancient Chinese religion mainly consists in a morality like of Plato, Marcus Aurelius, Epictetus, and all our philosophers. The Chinese emperor never paid debaters to know if an infant was damned when it died before it had taken a breath, if a third person was made or engendered or proceeded, if it proceeded from a first person or from a second or from both at the same time, if one of these persons had two natures or only one, if it had one will or two, if the mother of one of these persons was stained or unstained. They didn't know consubstantiability or consubstantiation. The forty Chinese parliaments that govern the whole empire know nothing of all this; therefore, they are atheists! That's how Christians have always argued. When will they start reasoning?

It is a very strange abuse of people's stupidity; it is very stupid in itself or very dishonest and mean just to want to make people believe that the principle part of religion is not morality. To worship God and be just, that's the only religion of the lettered Chinese. Their canonical books, which they say are almost forty thousand years old, command the emperor to plow some furrows with his own hands and offer to the Supreme Being the ears of wheat produced by his work. O Thomas Aquinas, Scotus, Bonaventura, Francis, Dominic, Luther, Calvin, canons of Westminster, teach something better!

This simple and noble religion has lasted four thousand years in all its integrity and it is probably a lot older. For, seeing that the great emperor Fo-Hi, whom the most moderate compilers place in the time when we place the Flood, observed this august ceremony of sowing wheat, it is very likely that it was established long before him. Otherwise wouldn't they have said that he instituted it? Fo-Hi was at the head of countless people, so this assembled nation was far older than Fo-Hi; therefore, it had a religion for a long time. For, what great people were ever without religion? There is no example on earth.

But what is unique and admirable is that in China the emperor was always pontiff and preacher. The edicts were always exhortations to virtue. The emperor always sacrificed to Tien and Chang-Ti. There was no priest insolent enough to tell him, "I am the only one who can sacrifice and pray to God in public. Touch the censer, dare to pray to God yourselves, you are impious."

The lower classes were stupid and superstitious in China as elsewhere. They worshipped ridiculous gods in later times; they raised up many sects for around three thousand years. The wise and tolerant government let them survive, caring only about morality and order; it did not find it harmful that the rabble believed inanities provided that it did not trouble the state and it obeyed the laws. The maxim of this government was always "Believe what you want but do what I tell you."

During the beginning of our common era, some wretch named Fo claimed to be born out of the left side of a white elephant and his disciples made this poor charlatan a god. The forty great parliaments of the kingdom allowed the populace to entertain themselves with this farce. No popular stupidities troubled the state; they did no more harm than the *Metamorphoses* of Ovid and the *Golden Ass* of Apuleius did in Rome. But us, wretched us! What inanities, what stupidities, what trouble, and what carnage! Chinese history was sullied with no religious trouble. No prophet stirred up the people; no mystery ravaged their souls. Confucius was the leader among doctors because he was never a quack. But us, wretched us!

Chapter 5

On India, Brahmins, and Their Theology, Imitated Very Late by the Jews and Then by the Christians

The religion of the Brahmins is even more ancient than the Chinese, at least the Brahmins say so. They preserve a book that they claim was written more than three thousand years before our common era in the language of Sanskrit, which some people still understand. No one, at least among the modern Brahmins, doubts that this book, so sacred to them, is much older than the Vedas, so famous in antiquity. The book I'm talking about is called the *Shasta*. It was the rule of the Indians for 1,500 years until the Brahmins became more powerful and gave the Vedas as rule, a new book based on the ancient *Shasta*, so that the people had a first and second law. (See the book of Holwell, who lived among the Brahmins for thirty years.)

The first law of the Indians seemed to be the origin of the theology of many nations. It is in the *Shasta* that you find the Supreme Being who ordered the chaos and formed the celestial creatures. These demigods revolted against the great God who banished them from their residence for many centuries. And it is remarkable that half of the demigods remained faithful to their sovereign.

It is clearly this that later gave rise to the Greeks' fable of giants fighting against Zeus, the master of the gods. Hercules and other gods sided with Zeus. The defeated giants were enchained.

Let's notice here that the Jews, who only formed a body of people many centuries after the Indians, had no idea of this theological mystery. There is no trace of it in Genesis. It was only in the first century of our era that a very clumsy forger, either a Jew or a half-Jew, half-Christian, having learned something of the Brahmins' religion, fabricated a book that he dared to attribute to Enoch. It is in this book of Enoch that is mentioned the rebellion of some celestial powers that the forger called angels. Semexiah, he said, was their leader. Araciel and Chababiel were his lieutenant generals. The faithful angels were Michael, Raphael, Gabriel, and Uriel. In the end it was on the mumbo jumbo of this so-called book of Enoch that Milton built his curious poem about Paradise lost. That's how all fables have made their way around the world.

What sensible reader won't notice today without astonishment that the Christian religion was solely founded on this fall of angels, of which no mention was made in the Old Testament? They attribute to Simon Barjone, called Peter, a letter in which they made him say that "God did not spare the angels who sinned but threw them into Tartarus with the cables of hell" (2 Pet. 2:4). We do not know if by "sinner angels" the author meant the rulers of the earth and if by "sinners" he meant the celestial spirits who revolted against God. And it is also very surprising that Simon Barjone, who was born in Galilee, knew Tartarus.

In short, it is only in four lines attributed to Simon Barjone that we find some feeble idea of the fall of the angels, of this first foundation of the entire Christian religion.

Since then they have concluded that the captain of these rebel angels-become-devils was Lucifer. Why? Because the star of Venus, the morning star, was sometimes called Lucifer in Latin. They found a parable against the king of Babylon in Isaiah. Isaiah himself called this rhetorical apostrophe a parable. He called this king and his henchmen the "iron rod," the "scepter of the impious." He said the cedars and pines were rejoicing over the death of this king. He said that the giants congratulated him when he arrived in hell. "How you have fallen from heaven," he said, "you who were like the star of Venus and rose in the morning. How you have fallen to earth, you who struck down nations," etc. [Isa. 14:12].

Translators liked to render the passage thus: "How you have

fallen from heaven, Lucifer." The commentators have not failed to conclude that this passage was addressed to the devil, that the devil was Lucifer, that it was he who revolted against God, that it was he who is in hell forever, that it was he who persuaded Eve to eat the fruit of the knowledge of good and evil in order to have partners, that he thus damned the human race and that the constitution of our religion revolves around Lucifer. O great power of ambiguity!

The allegory of the angels revolting against God was originally an Indian parable that had a long life afterward in almost all the West under a hundred different disguises.

Chapter 6

On Metempsychosis, Burning Widows, Francis Xavier, and Warburton

T he Indians are the first people who showed an inventive spirit. We can assess this by the games of chess and backgammon, by the numbers that we owe to them, and finally by the travels that since time immemorial we have made there for education as well as for commerce.

They made the mistake of mixing up with their inventions some superstitions that were ridiculous and others that were abominable. The idea of a soul distinct from the body, the eternity of this soul, and metempsychosis are their inventions. These are, no doubt, lovely ideas, with more sense in them than in the *Utopia* and the *Argenis* and even than in the *Thousand and One Nights*. Above all, the doctrine of metempsychosis is neither absurd nor useless.

Since they admire souls, they see how impertinent it would be for the Supreme Being to continually be busy creating new ones as animals mate. This would be putting God eternally on the lookout to quickly form a new spirit at the very moment that the seed of a male body is shot into the womb of a female body. He would have a lot to deal with if he had to create souls all at once for all the trysts of our world, not counting the others, and what would become of these souls when the fetus died? This, however, is the opinion or rather the vain discourse of our theologians. They say that God creates a soul for every fetus but only at the end of six weeks. What's more ridiculous than that; the Brahmins' was more ingenious. Souls are eternal; they pass constantly from one body to another. If your soul was vicious in the body of a tyrant, it will be condemned to enter into a wolf who will be constantly chased by dogs and whose hide will be used as clothing for a shepherd.

There is intelligence and equity in this old system. But why are there so many vain ceremonies to which the Brahmins subject themselves during their life? Why hold a cow by the tail when dying? And especially, why for three thousand years have Indian widows made it a point of honor to burn themselves with the bodies of their husbands?

I have read from cover to cover the rites of the new and old Brahmins in the book of the *Cormo Vedam*. They are only tiring ceremonies and mystical ideas of contemplation and the union with God, but I saw nothing that had the slightest relation to the tail of a cow that sanctifies the Indians in death. Nor did I read a single word concerning the precept or counsel given to widows to burn themselves on the pyres of their spouses. Apparently these two ancient customs, the former eccentric and the latter horrid, were first practiced by some hollow brain; and other brains more hollow still outdid it. One woman tore out her hair and bruised her face when her husband died. A second wounded herself. A third burned herself and before burning herself she gave money to the priests, who didn't fail to urge women to follow such a lovely example. Soon it was shameful not to be burned. All appalling customs had pretty much the same origin. The lawmakers are usually men with enough common sense to order nothing that is too absurd and too contrary to nature. They only make a particular practice more fashionable when it has already been accepted. Mohammed did not invent circumcision, but found it established. He himself had been circumcised. Numa did not order anything impertinent or appalling. We do not read that Minos gave ridiculous precepts to the Cretans, but there are people more enthusiastic than others who exaggerate and disfigure all the precepts of the first lawmakers; we have terrible examples among us. Eccentric and barbaric practices are established by themselves; we can only leave the people alone.

What is very remarkable is that these same Brahmins, who were of such remote antiquity, are the only priests in the world who have preserved both their ancient dogmas and their authority. They still form the first tribe, the highest caste from the river Ganges to the coasts of Coromandel and Malabar. In the past they governed. Their present ceremonies still bear witness to this. The *Cormo Vedam* ordains that at the birth of a Brahmin, they solemnly say, "Live to command men."

They have preserved their ancient emblems. Our famous Holwell, who lived with them for thirty years, has given us the stamps of their hieroglyphs. Virtue is represented here mounted on a dragon. It has ten arms to withstand the ten principle vices. It is especially this figure that the Papist missionaries didn't fail to take for the devil, so fair and wise were these gentlemen.

Bishop Warburton assures us that the Jesuit Xavier in one of his letters claims that a Brahmin told him in secret about his friends: "It is true that there is a God and our idols are only representations of evil spirits, but beware telling the people. Politicians want to keep them in ignorance of all divinity." Xavier had little common sense and a great deal of gall when he wrote such a huge stupidity. I will not examine how he could have made himself capable of conversing so familiarly in the language of Malabar in such a short time and of being on such intimate terms with a Brahmin who should have defied him, but it is not possible that this Brahmin had slandered himself so shamefully. It is even less possible that he said that for political reasons they had to make people atheists. It is precisely the opposite: Francis Xavier, the apostle of India, either very much misunderstood or he lied. But it is Warburton who misread and misreported what he read, which happens very often.

Here, word for word, is what Xavier said in the collection of his selected letters, printed in French at Warsaw by Veidman in 1739, page 36 and 37:

> A learned Brahmin . . . told me as a great secret firstly that the scholars of this university made the students swear to never reveal their mysteries, but that he would reveal them to me thanks to the friendship he felt toward me. One of these mysteries is that there is only one God, creator of heaven and earth, whom they have to worship: for the idols are only representations of demons; and that the Brahmins have certain dissertations like memorials of their holy

Scripture in which they maintain that the divine laws are contained and which the masters use when teaching, in a language unknown to the common people, like Latin among us. He explained to me very clearly these divine precepts, one after another, which would be too long and irrelevant for me write here. The sages celebrate Sunday as a holiday and from time to time they make this prayer in their language: "My God, I worship you and implore your help forever," which they often repeat in a whisper because they have sworn to keep it a secret. . . . Finally, he begged me to teach him the principle mysteries of the Christian religion, promising to never speak of them. . . . I only explained to him carefully that saying of Jesus Christ that contains a summary of our faith: "Whoever believes and is baptized, will be saved" [Mark 16:16].

This letter is much more curious than Warburton, who falsified it, thinks. First of all, we see that the Brahmins worship a Supreme God and are not idolaters. Secondly, the Brahmins' expression of prayer is admirable. Thirdly, the expression that Xavier opposes has nothing to do with it and is very poorly applied. The Brahmin says he must worship, the other says he must believe and adds that he must be baptized. The religion of the Brahmin is of the heart; the apostle converter's is the religion of ceremonies and, moreover, this converter of souls had to have been very ignorant not to know that baptism was one of the ancient customs of India and it preceded ours by several centuries. We could say that it was up to the Brahmin to convert Xavier and that this Xavier was bound to fail at converting the Brahmin.

The farther we advance in knowledge of the nations that people the earth, the more we see that almost all of them have a Supreme God. We made peace two years ago in Carolina with the Cherokees; the chief, whom we call Little Carpenter, said these words to colonel Grant: "The English are whiter than us, but a single God is our common father. The all-powerful created all people and he loves them equally."

This speech of Little Carpenter is far above all barbaric and impious dogmatists who say, "There is only one chosen people who can please God!"

Chapter 7

On the Chaldeans

We cannot be astonished enough at the 1,903 years of astronomical observations that the Chaldeans handed over to Alexander.

This series, which dates back to around 2,250 years before our era, necessarily assumes a tremendous antiquity preceding it. I have mentioned elsewhere that for a nation to cultivate astronomy, it must have gone centuries without cultivating it. The Romans had a limited knowledge of the sphere only in the time of Cicero. However, they were able to have recourse to the Greeks for a long time. The Chaldeans owed their knowledge only to themselves. Therefore, this knowledge came very late. They had to perfect all the mechanical arts before having a college of astronomers. Now, if we grant that this college was established only two thousand years before Alexander, which is a very short time, will it be too much to give two thousand years for the establishment of other arts before the establishment of this college?

Certainly, it takes more than two thousand years for men (as we have often observed) to invent a language, an alphabet, to form the art of writing, to master metals. Thus, if we say that the Chaldeans had at least four thousand years of antiquity at the time of Alexander, it will be very prudent and moderate. They had an era then of 470,000 years. We are cutting away from them 466,000 years in one fell swoop: this is very harsh. But, they'll tell us, despite this huge deduction it is found that the Chaldeans were already a powerful people one thousand years before our Flood. This is not my fault; I can't help it. Let's begin by giving you your Flood that your Hebrew Bible, that the Samaritans, that the so-called Septuagint places in epochs differing by about seven hundred years. You give more than sixty systems to your chronology and then you mock the Chaldeans.

What was the religion of the Chaldeans before the Persians conquered Babylon and before the doctrine of Zoroaster was mixed up with that of the mages of Chaldea? It was Sabism, the adoration of a God and the veneration of the stars considered in one part of the East as subordinate gods.

There is no religion in which we do not see a Supreme God at the head of everything. There is also no religion that wasn't instituted to make men less wicked.

I do not see why Chaldeism, Sabism, could have been considered idolatry. In the first place, a star is not an idol, an image—it is a sun like ours. Second, why not venerate God in these admirable works by which we regulate our seasons and our labor? Third, the entire earth believed that our destinies depended on the arrangement of the constellations. Assuming this error and that the mages were unfortunately astrologers by profession, it was really forgivable in them for offering some prayers to these great luminous bodies in which the power of the great Being manifested itself with so much majesty. The stars are every bit as good as St. Roch, St. Pancras, St. Fiacre, St. Ursula, and St. Potamienne whose alleged bones the Roman Catholics worship on their knees. The planets are every bit as good as the pieces of rotten wood that they call the true cross. Once again let the Papists not mock anyone; and let us be on guard also. For, if we are better than they are, it's not by much.

The Chaldean mages taught virtue just like all the other priests and didn't practice it more.

Chapter 8

On the Persians and Zoroastrians

While the Chaldeans were so well aware of the virtue of the stars and were teaching, as the *Almanac of Liege* has done since, on what day we should clip our nails, the ancient Persians were not so clever. They worshipped a God like the Chaldeans and revered fire as the emblem of the Divinity.

Whether this worship was taught by a Zerdust, whom the Greeks (who changed all Asian names) called Zoroaster a long time afterward, or whether there were many Zoroasters, or whether there were any, at least it is certain that the Persians were the first to hold fire sacred and admit a place of delights for the just and a hell for the wicked, a good principle that was God and an evil principle from which the devil came to us. This evil principle, Ahriman, Satan, was neither God nor coeternal with God, but in the end it existed. And it was very natural to admit an evil principle seeing that there are so many evil effects.

The Persians at first had no temple, no altar; they only had them when they were integrated with the Babylonians whom they conquered, like the Franks only did when they had subjugated the Gauls. These ancient Persians only held fire sacred in remote caves; they called it Vesta.

This worship passed to other nations a long time afterward. It was finally introduced among the Romans who took Vesta for a goddess. Almost all the ancient ceremonies were established on mistakes.

When the Persians conquered the kingdom of Babylon, the religion of the conquerors mixed with that of the conquered and even greatly prevailed, but the Chaldeans always remained in possession of telling fortunes.

It is unquestionable that both believed in the immortality of the soul without knowing what it was any better than we do. Although we have proofs of this in the book of Sadder, which contains the ancient Persian doctrine, it would be convincing enough just to glance at the ruins of Persepolis of which we have many very precise drawings. Here we see tombs from which heads stick out, each one accompanied by a pair of extended wings; they are all taking flight toward heaven.

Of all the religions that we have covered up to here, only the Chinese do not admit the immortality of the soul. And notice that these ancient religions still survive. That of the government of China has been preserved in all its integrity; that of the Brahmins still dominates in the Indian peninsula; that of Zoroaster has not been denied, although its followers have been dispersed.

Chapter 9

On the Phoenicians and Sanchuniathon, before the Time of Moses

The peoples of Phoenicia cannot be as old as the peoples we have spoken of. They lived on the Mediterranean coast and this coast was very sterile. It is true that this sterility itself came in useful for the grandeur of these peoples. They were forced into maritime trade, which made them rich. These new brokers of Asia penetrated into Africa, Spain, and all the way to our England. Sidon, Tyre, Biblos, Berytus became opulent cities, but Syria, Chaldea, and Persia had to have already been very important states before the Phoenicians attempted seafaring. For, why would they have undertaken such dangerous travels if they hadn't had such rich neighbors to whom they could sell the productions of their remote country? Nevertheless, the Tyrians had a temple that Herodotus entered and that he said was 2,300 years old. So it had been built around 2,800 years before our common era; thus, by this calculation the temple of Tyre existed nearly 1,800 years before that of Solomon (using the calculation of the Vulgate).

Since the Phoenicians were great businessmen, they necessarily cultivated the art of writing. They kept records, had archives; their country was even called "the country of letters." It is proven that they passed their alphabet on to the Greeks and when the Jews came to establish themselves within their boundaries a long time afterward, these foreigners took their alphabet and their writing. Even in the history of Joshua you will find that on the border of Phoenicia, in the country called Canaan only by the Jews, there was a city that they called "the City of Letters, the City of Books, Cariath Sepher," which was taken and almost destroyed by the brigand Othoniel, to whom the brigand Caleb, partner of the brigand Joshua, gave his daughter Oxa as a reward (Judg. 1:11; cf. Josh. 15:15).

One of the most curious monuments of antiquity is without a doubt the History of Sanchuniathon the Phoenician, of which there remains some precious fragments preserved in Eusebius. It is incontestable that this author wrote a long time before the eruption of the Hebrews into the country of Canaan. An irrefutable proof of this is that he does not talk about the Hebrews. If they had already come among the Canaanites, if they had put the country of Sanchuniathon to fire and sword, if in the vicinity they had exerted cruelties of which there were hardly any examples in ancient history, it is impossible that Sanchuniathon would have passed over in silence such events that should have interested him greatly. If there had been a Moses before him, it is certain that he would not have forgotten this Moses and the horrific prodigies performed in Egypt. Therefore, he obviously preceded the time of Moses. He therefore wrote his cosmogony long before the Jews had their Genesis.

Besides, you shouldn't be astonished to find in this Phoenician's cosmogony no names cited in the Jewish Genesis. No writer or people knew the names Adam, Cain, Abel, Enoch, Methuselah, or Noah. If only one of these names had been cited by Sanchuniathon or by some writer in Syria, Chaldea, or Egypt, the historian Josephus would not have failed to boast about it. He himself said in his *Against Apion* that he had consulted all the foreign authors who spoke about his nation and, as hard as he tried, he couldn't find a single one who spoke about the miracles of Moses, not a single one who called to mind a word of Genesis or Exodus.

Let's add to these convincing proofs that if there had been a single word in Sanchuniathon or in some other foreign author on behalf of Jewish history, Eusebius, who made weapons of everything, in his *Preparation of the Gospel*, would have emphatically cited this evidence. But this is no place to extend this research; it is enough to show that Sanchuniathon wrote in his language long before the Jews could even pronounce theirs.

What again makes the fragments of Sanchuniathon very commendable is that he consulted the wisest priests of his country, among whom were Jerombal, priest of Iaho in the city of Berytus. This name Iaho, which means God, is the sacred name that was long afterward adopted by the Jews.

The work of Sanchuniathon is even more worthy of the entire world's attention because his cosmogony is taken (according to his own statement) from the books of the Thoth, king of Egypt, who had lived, he says, eight hundred years before and whom the Greeks called Mercury since then. We hardly have any evidence of greater antiquity. This is indisputably the greatest monument that remains to us in the West.

Some timid souls, frightened by this antiquity and by this monument that is so much earlier than Genesis, had no other recourse but to say that these fragments were counterfeit. But this poor evasion is blasted by the pains that Eusebius took to transcribe them. He fights against their principles but avoids fighting against their authenticity; it was too well known in his time. The book was translated into Greek by a citizen of Sanchuniathon's own country. With as little as it would take to doubt the authenticity of this book opposed to the Bible in everything, Eusebius would no doubt have done it with all his strength. He did not do it. What proof is more dazzling than the admission of an adversary? Therefore, we admit without difficulty that Sanchuniathon is much older than any Jewish book.

The religion of these Phoenicians was, like all the others, a healthy morality, because it can't have two moralities in it—one metaphysically absurd, like all metaphysics until Locke, and ridiculous rites because the people have always loved mummeries. When I say that all religions have affectations unworthy of honest people, I always make an exception for that of the Chinese government that no gross superstition has ever sullied.

The Phoenicians firstly recognized a chaos as had the Indians. The spirit became enamored of the principles mixed up in the chaos, it united with them and love disentangled everything. The earth, the stars, the animals were born.

These same Phoenicians sacrificed to the winds and this superstition was very fitting to a seafaring people. Every city of Phoenicia later had its own gods and rites.

The worship of the goddess whom we call Venus came especially from Phoenicia. The fable of Venus and Adonis is entirely Phoenician. Adonis or Adonai was one of their gods and when the Jews came into the vicinity much later, they called their god by the Phoenician names, Jehovah, Iaho, Adonai, Shaddai, and so on.

The whole country from Tyre to the heart of Arabia is the cradle of fables, as we shall see below. And it was bound to be so since it was the country of letters.

Chapter 10

On the Egyptians

The French poet-philosopher who first said that the Egyptians were a brand new nation based himself on an irrefutable reason: it is that Egypt was inundated five months of the year and these successive inundations had to make the miry land entirely impractical, that it took centuries to tame the Nile, to dig canals, construct cities twenty feet above the ground; that Asia, on the other hand, had immense plains, more favorable rivers, and, consequently, that all the Asian peoples were bound to form civilized societies long before they could build a single bearable house next to the Nile.

But the antiquity of the pyramids are so remote that it's unknown! But Thoth gave laws to Egypt eight hundred years before Sanchuniathon, who lived long before the eruption of the Jews into Palestine! But the Greeks and Romans revered the antiquities of Egypt. Yes, all this proves that the Egyptian government is much older than ours. But this government was modern compared to Asian peoples.

I disregard those few unfortunates who lived between the rocks that border the Nile just like I make no mention of our barbaric predecessors who lived for so long in our wild forests before being civilized. A nation exists only when it has laws and arts. The state of the savage is the state of a brute. Civilized Egypt is therefore very modern; to such an extent that they took from the Phoenicians the name of Iaho, a cabalistic name that the priests gave to God.

But without entering into these obscure discussions, let's limit ourselves to our subject, which is to find out if all these great nations acknowledged a Supreme God. It is incontestable that this doctrine was the foundation of the whole Egyptian theology. This is proven by the ineffable name itself of Iaho, which means the Eternal, by the globe that was set on the door of the temples and that represented the unity of the great Being under the name of Knef. It is proven above all by what remains to us of the mysteries of Isis and that ancient litany preserved in Apuleius, "The celestial powers serve you, the underworld submits to you, the universe turns under your hand, your feet trample Tartarus, the stars answer to your voice, the seasons return at your command, the elements obey you!"

Never was the unity of a Supreme God more strongly pronounced. And why did they say that the celestial powers obeyed, that the stars answered to the voice of the high priest? It is because the stars, the supposed spirits scattered in space, were considered secondary gods, beings superior to men and inferior to God—a familiar doctrine throughout the East, a doctrine finally adopted in Greece and Italy.

As for the immortality of the soul, no one ever doubted that it was one of the two great principles of the religion of Egypt. The pyramids vouch for this well enough. The rulers of the country raised these enduring tombs and embalmed their bodies so carefully only so that the spirit of fire or air, which they always supposed animated the body, could regain the body at the end of one thousand years; some even say at the end of three thousand years. Nothing proves so well that the belief in the immortality of the soul was established in Egypt.

I won't speak here about the foolish and ridiculous superstitions with which this pleasant country was inundated much more than with the waters of its river. It became the most despicable of great peoples, just as the Jews have become the most despicable and disgraceful of little nations. My only objective is to show that the great civilized peoples, and even the little ones, have recognized a Supreme God since time immemorial and that all great peoples explicitly admitted the after death persistence of what we call soul, except the Chinese. Still, we cannot say that the Chinese formally denied it. They neither affirmed it nor fought against it. Were they wiser or simply ignorant in this?

Chapter 11

On the Arabs and Bacchus

Herodotus teaches us that the Arabs worshipped Venus-Urania and Bacchus. But what part of Arabia is he talking about? It is probably all three. Alexander, he says, wanted to establish the seat of his empire in Arabia Felix. He sent word to the people of Yemen and Saana that he had done as much as Bacchus and he wanted to be worshipped like him. Now, it is very likely that Bacchus was worshipped in greater Arabia as well as in Arabia Petraea and the Desert. The poor provinces always conform themselves to the customs of the rich. But how did the Arabs worship Venus? They worshipped the stars while, however, acknowledging a Supreme God. And it is so true that they worshipped the Supreme Being that from time immemorial they divided their fields into two. The first was for God and the second for the star that they were so fond of (see the preface to the Koran by Sale). Allah was always the name of God among them. The neighboring peoples pronounced it El. Thus Babel on the Euphrates was the City of God, Israel among the Persians meant "Seeing God," and the Hebrews took this name Israel afterward, as the Jew Philo admits. All the names of Persian angels ended in El: Messenger of God, Soldier of God, Friend of God. The Jews even added the Persian name El to the Phoenician names of God Iaho, Adonai, from which they made Eloi or Eloa.

But how did the Arabs worship Venus-Urania? Venus is a Latin word; Urania is Greek. The Arabs surely knew neither Greek nor Latin, and they were incomparably older than the peoples of Greece and Italy. Also, the Arab name they used to signify the star Venus was Alilat; and Mercury was Atarid, and so forth.

The only man to whom they granted divine honors was he whom the Greeks later called Bacchus, his Arabic name was Bac or Urotal or Misem. He will be the only deified man of whom I'll speak, given the tremendous similarity there is between him and the Moses of the Hebrews.

This Arab Bacchus was born, like Moses, in Egypt and was raised in Arabia around Mount Sinai, which the Arabs called Nisa. He crossed the Red Sea with his army without wetting his feet to conquer India and there were many women in this army. He made a fountain of wine spring forth from a rock by striking it with his thyrsus. He stopped the sun and moon in their course. He brought forth rays of light from his head. Finally, they called him Misem, which is one the names of Moses and means "saved from the waters" because they claimed that he fell into the sea in his infancy. All these Arab fables were handed down to the first Greeks, and Orpheus sang his adventures. Nothing is as old as this fable. Perhaps it is an allegory. No people have ever invented more parables than the Arabs. They usually wrote them in verse. Every year they gathered together in a large square in Ocad (see the preface to the wonderful English translation of the Koran) where they held a month-long fair. They gave a prize to the poet who recited the most extraordinary story. The story of Bacchus was no doubt based on reality.

Chapter 12

On the Greeks, Socrates, and the Double Doctrine

So much has been said about the Greeks that I will have little to say. I will only mention that they worshipped a Supreme God and acknowledged the immortality of the soul, following the example of the Asians and Egyptians, not only before they had historians, but before Homer wrote. Homer invented nothing about the gods; he took them as they were. Orpheus had got his theogony accepted in Greece long before him. In this theogony everything starts with chaos like with the Phoenicians and Persians. A supreme artisan orders the chaos and forms the sun, the moon, the stars, and the earth out of it. This Supreme Being called Zeus, Jupiter, is the master of all the other gods, the god of gods. You see this theogony everywhere in Homer. Jupiter alone assembles the council; he alone casts thunder; he commands all the gods, rewards them, and punishes them; he chases Apollo from heaven; he scolds Juno, fastens her between heaven and earth with a golden chain; but Homer does not say from which fixed point this chain was hung. The same Jupiter pushed Vulcan from the top of heaven onto the earth; he threatened the god Mars. In the end, he is the master everywhere.

Nothing is clearer in Homer than the ancient opinion about the immortality of the soul, even though nothing is more obscure than its existence. What is the soul among the ancient poets and all the philosophers? It is something that animates the body, a nimble figure, a little thing composed of air that looks like the human body and escapes when it has lost its envelope. Ulysses finds thousands of them in Hades. The boatman Charon is continually busy with transporting them in his boat. This theology is as ridiculous as the rest, I agree, but it proves that the immortality of the soul was a major point among the ancients.

This did not prevent entire sects of philosophers from mocking both Jupiter and the immortality of the soul. And we should carefully observe that the sect of Epicurus, which we can consider a society of atheists, was always very honored. I say that it was a society of atheists because when it comes to religion and morality, to suppose that the gods are useless and do not punish or reward and to suppose nothing at all is the same thing.

Why, then, were the Epicurians never persecuted and Socrates was sentenced to drink hemlock? There absolutely had to be another reason than fanaticism to condemn Socrates. The Epicureans were the friendliest men in the world and Socrates seemed to have been the unfriendliest. He himself admitted in his defense that he went from door to door in Athens to prove to people that they were stupid. He made so many enemies that they finally managed to sentence him to death, after which they asked his forgiveness. This is precisely (except for the forgiveness) the experience of Vanini. He argued bitterly in Toulouse against the judges. They convinced him that he was an atheist and a sorcerer and they burned him as a result. These horrors are more common among the Christians than in ancient Greece.

Bishop Warburton in his very strange book *The Divine Legation of Moses* (vol. 2, book 3) claims that the philosophers who taught the immortality of the soul did not at all believe in it. He tries everything possible to prove that the ancient sages had a double doctrine, one public and one secret, that they preached in public the immortality of the soul to satisfy the stupid people and that they mocked all of this privately with intelligent men. That, I confess, is a peculiar assertion for a bishop. But why did these philosophers need to say aloud what they did not believe in secret, seeing that it was permitted to the Epicureans to say out loud that everything perished with the body and the Pyrrhonians could doubt everything with impunity? Who could have forced the philosophers to lie in the morning in order to speak truth in the evening? Some scoundrels in Greece, as elsewhere, could have exploited the words of the sage and brought a lawsuit against him. They arraigned members of parliament for their words, but this does not prove that the House of Commons had two different doctrines.

This double doctrine that our Warburton wants to talk about was mainly in the mysteries of Isis, Ceres, and Orpheus and not among the philosophers. They taught the unity of God in these mysteries while in public they sacrificed to ridiculous gods. That is an incontestable truth. All the expressions of the mysteries attest to the worship of a single God. It is exactly as if there were congregations of wise men among the Papists who, after having attended the mass of St. Ursula and the eleven thousand virgins, of St. Roch and his dog, of St. Anthony and his pig, afterward went to deny these astonishing stupidities in a private gathering; but, on the contrary, the brotherhood of Papists still outdo the superstitions forced on them. Their penitents cloaked in white, grey, and black whip themselves in honor of these lovely saints instead of worshipping God in reasonable men.

To prove that the Greeks had two doctrines, one for the Areopagus and the other for their friends, Warburton cites Caesar, Cato, and Cicero who said in the open Senate during the trial of Cataline that death was not an evil, that it was the end of all sensations and there was nothing after us. But Caesar, Cato, and Cicero were not Greeks. Did they explain their secret doctrine to three or four hundred of their confidants in the open Senate?

This bishop could have added that in Seneca's tragedy *The Trojan Women* the chorus secretly spoke to the assembled people of Rome:

Post mortem nihil est, ipsaque mors nihil.
Quaeris quo iacent post obitum loco?
Quo non nata iacent?

After death there is nothing, death itself is nothing.
Do you ask where they are after death?
Where are the unborn? (*Troades*, 387, 407–408)

When they made Warburton conscious of all these impertinences and discrepancies of his, he was angry—he didn't answer reasonably or politely, he was like those women who are caught in the act and become bolder and meaner: "There is nothing bolder than those who are caught red-handed" (Juvenal, *Satires*, 6.284). The ardor of his courage carried him even further, as we shall see when dealing with the Jewish religion.

Chapter 13

On the Romans

L et us be as brief with the Romans as we were with the Greeks. It is the same religion, the same principal gods, the same Jupiter, master of gods and men, the same Elysian Fields, the same Tartarus, the same apotheoses. And though the sect of Epicurus had a very great reputation, though they publicly mocked the auguries, haruspices, Elysian Fields, and Hades, the Roman religion survived until the fall of the empire.

It is unquestionable by all their expressions that the Romans recognized a single Supreme God. They gave only to Jupiter the title of very great and very good, *optimus maximus*. Lightning was only in his hands. All the other gods can be compared to the saints and the Virgin that Italy worships today. In short, the more we learn about civilized peoples, the more we find a God everywhere, as I have already said.

Our Warburton, whose sense is always the enemy of the common sense of other men, dares to assure us in the preface to the second part of his *Divine Legation* that the Romans did not respect Jupiter very much. He wants to rely on the authority of Cicero; he claims that the orator said in his defense of Flaccus "that the majesty of the Empire has nothing to do with the acknowledgment of a single God." He cites the Latin words *majestatem imperii non decuisse ut unus tantum*

Deus colatur. Who would believe it? There is not a word of this in the defense of Flaccus or in any other speech that has the slightest relation to this so-called citation of Cicero. It belongs entirely to our bishop who wanted to deceive the world through this fraud, and not a pious fraud but a shameful one. He figured that no one would take the time to leaf through Cicero and discover his imposture; he fooled himself in this as in everything else and henceforth we will put no more faith in his commentaries on Cicero than on those he gave us on Shakespeare.

What is perhaps most respectable about the Romans is that for nine hundred years they persecuted no one for their opinions. They cannot be reproached for hemlock. They were the most universally tolerant people. These wise conquerors besieged a city; they prayed to the gods of the city to be kind enough to pass over their camp. When it was taken, they went to sacrifice in the temple of the conquered. That is how they became worthy of commanding so many nations.

We did not see them slaughter the Tuscans to reform the art of the haruspices, which they got from them. No one died in Rome for having spoken badly about the sacred chickens. The Egyptians, covered in scorn, had a temple of Isis in Rome; the even more despised Jews had synagogues there after their bloody rebellions. The conquering people were the tolerant people.

It must be admitted that they mistreated the Christians only after these newcomers loudly and repeatedly declared that they could allow no other worship but theirs. That is what we will clearly show when we come to the founding of Christianity.

Let's begin by examining the Jewish religion, from which Christianity and the Mohammedans came.

Chapter 14

On the Jews and Their Origin

All nations (except, as always, for the Chinese) boast about a bunch of oracles and prodigies, but everything is prodigy and oracle in the Jewish history without exception. So much has been written on the matter that nothing is left to discover. I do not want to repeat all the constant miracles or fight against them; I respect the mother of our religion. I will speak about the Judaic marvels only insofar as it can be used to establish the facts. I will examine this history like the history of Livy or Herodotus. Let us use only the lights of reason to search for what the Jews were, where they came from when they set themselves up in Palestine, when their religion was settled, when they wrote. Let us educate ourselves and try not to make a scandal of the weaknesses, which is not very easy when you want to tell the truth.

We barely find more light shed by foreigners on the little Hebrew nation than we find on the Franks, Irish, and Basques. All the Egyptian books have perished; their language has suffered the same fate. We no longer have the Persian, Chaldean, and Syrian authors to educate us. We are traveling here in a desert where wild animals lived. Let's try to discover some of their footprints.

Were the Jews originally a wandering horde of Arabs from the desert, who spread out between Egypt and Syria, were multiplied and took hold of some towns around Phoenicia? Nothing is more likely. Their temperament, their taste for parables and incredible marvels, their extreme passion for thievery—all this leads us to consider them a very newly established nation that emerged from a little Arab horde.

There's more: In their history they claim that they and the Arab tribes descended from the same father, that the children of some wandering shepherds named Abraham, Lot, and Esau inhabited the regions of Arabia. Now there's some speculation for you; but there is no monument left to support it.

If we examine this important case only with common sense, we cannot consider the Jewish books as proofs. They are not judges in their own cause. I do not believe Livy when he tells us that Romulus was the son of the god Mars; I do not believe our first English writers when they say that Vortigern was a wizard; I do not believe the old histories of the Franks that date their origin back to Francus, son of Hector. I shouldn't believe the Jews on their word alone when they say such extraordinary things. I am speaking here according to my human faith and I am very careful not to infringe upon divine faith. Therefore, I will look elsewhere for some weak light by which I might discover the beginnings of the Jewish nation.

More than one ancient writer says that it was a leprous group that was chased from Egypt by King Amasis. This is only an assumption. It acquired a certain degree of probability by the admission of the Jews themselves that they fled Egypt and were highly prone to leprosy. But these two degrees of probability, the consent of many ancients and the admission of the Jews, are still far from establishing certainty.

Diodorus Siculus, following the Egyptian writers he consulted, records that the same Amasis waged war with Aktisanes, king of Ethiopia, who conquered and cut off the noses and ears of a horde of thieves who had infested Egypt during the war. He confined this band of thieves to the desert of Sinai, where they made the nets with which they caught quail to eat. They lived in this country that has since been called by a name that means "nose cut off" in Egyptian and that the Greeks called "Rhinocolure." This passage, which we have paid too little attention to, coupled with the ancient tradition that the Hebrews were a group of lepers chased from Egypt, seems to shed some light on their origin. They admit that they were both lepers and thieves; they say that after having robbed the Egyptians they fled into the very desert that was since called Rhinocolure. They specify that the sister of their Moses was a leper; they agree with the Egyptians on the matter of the quail.

Therefore, it is likely, humanly speaking and setting aside all the marvels, that the Jews were wandering Arabs prone to leprosy who sometimes came to pillage the borders of Egypt and who withdrew into the desert of Horeb and Sinai when their noses and ears were cut off. The hatred that they manifested against Egypt since then gives some force to this assumption. What again can increase the probability is that the Egyptian Apion of Alexandria, who wrote a history of his country at the time of Caligula, and another author named Chencres from the city of Mendes, both maintained that the Jews were chased out under the king or pharaoh Amasis. We have lost their writings, but the Jew Josephus, who wrote against Apion after his death, does not argue about the time of Amasis. He refutes him on other points: and all these other points prove that the Egyptians had written as many falsities about the Jews as they reproach the Jews themselves of having written.

Flavius Josephus was the only Jew who was considered by the Romans as having some common sense. However, this man of common sense reported in all seriousness the fable of the Septuagint and Aristaeus of which Van Dale and many others have shown the ridiculousness and absurdity. He adds to this nonsense that when the king of Egypt, Ptolemy Philadelphus, asked the translators how it could happen that books as wise as the Jews' had never been known to any nation, they answered him that these books were too divine for the profane to have ever dared to cite them and God could not permit it.

Notice how they make this lovely response at the very time they put these books into the hands of the profane. Josephus adds that all foreigners who had been bold enough to say something against the Jewish laws had been punished by God right away; that when the historian Theopompus had planned only to insert something from it into his work, he became crazy right away, but at the end of thirty days, after God had revealed to him in a dream that he could not speak about the Jews, he asked forgiveness of God and came back to his senses.

Josephus also says that when the poet Theodectes dared to speak about the Jews in one of his tragedies, he became blind right away and God gave him back his sight only after he had asked his forgiveness and repented.

If a man who is considered the only Jewish historian to have written reasonably told such enormous and trivial follies, what are we to think of the others? I am speaking always humanly, always putting myself in the place of a man who has never heard of the Jews or the Christians and was reading these books for the first time and, not having been illuminated by the light of grace, would be unfortunate enough to believe only his feeble reason while waiting to be enlightened from above.

Chapter 15

When Did the Jews Start Living in Cities, When Did They Write, and When Did They Have a Fixed and Permanent Religion?

Here we can consult the Jews themselves, compare what they record and see what is most probable.

According to them there were 630,000 soldiers living in tents in the desert, which makes around three million people at least, counting the elderly, women, and children. This strengthens the assumption that they were Arabs because they lived only in tents and moved around a lot. But how could three million people have had tents if they had fled from Egypt across the sea? Did each family carry their tent on their backs? They were not living in tents in Egypt. A proof that they were part of those wandering Arabs who loathe city dwellings is that when they seized Jericho, they razed it to the ground and settled nowhere. For, judging here only by the profane matters and using only the lights of reason, it is not for us to talk about the trumpets that brought down the walls of Jericho. That is one of those miracles that God performs all the time and that we dare not discuss.

Be that as it may, they say they did not have a capital city, were not settled in Jerusalem except in the time of David and, according to them, there were around 450 years between their flight from Egypt and their establishment in Jerusalem. I am not examining here their chronology in which they constantly contradict themselves, because in the best count there were more than six hundred years between Moses and

David. I see only that they lived in Palestine as wandering Arabs for many centuries, attacking all their neighbors one after another, pillaging everything, ravaging everything, sparing neither woman nor child, sometimes conquerors, sometimes conquered, and very often slaves.

Did this wandering life, this constant series of murders, this bloody exchange of victories and defeats, these long times of servitude allow them to learn to write and have a permanent religion? Isn't it much more likely that they began to form laws and written histories only under their kings and that beforehand they had only a vague and uncertain tradition?

Take a look at all Western nations from Archangel to Gibraltar: is there a single one that had laws and a written history before it was gathered together in cities? What I am saying is, are there any people on earth who had archives before being settled? How could the Jews alone have had this prerogative?

Chapter 16

What Was the Religion of the Jews at First?

We find in the book entitled Joshua these very words that the bloodthirsty chieftain said to the Jewish horde after capturing thirty-one villages and seizing their chiefs, called kings in the Bible (24:15–16): "Choose today whatever you want and see for yourselves whom you prefer to worship, whether the gods whom your fathers served in Mesopotamia or the gods of the Amorites in the country where you live, but as for me and my household we will serve Adonai. And the people answered: God would not like it if we abandon Adonai and serve other gods."

It is evident in this passage that Jews were assumed to have worshipped Isis and Osiris in Egypt and the stars in Mesopotamia. Joshua asks them whether they want to still worship the stars or Isis or Osiris, or Adonai the God of the Phoenicians where they were. Maybe he was a politician who understood very well that to adopt the God of the vanquished made them easier to govern. The barbarians who destroyed the Roman Empire, the Franks who sacked the Gauls, the Turks who subjugated the Mohammedan Arabs all had the prudence to embrace the religion of the conquered to accustom them more easily to servitude. But is it probable that such a little horde of Jewish barbarians had this policy?

Here is a second, very strong proof that these Jews did not yet have a fixed religion. It is that Jephthah, son of Gilead and a prostitute, elected captain of the wandering horde, said to the Moabites (Judges 11:24): "Does what your god Chemosh possess not belong to you? And what our god has obtained through his victories does it not belong to us?" Certainly it is evident that the Jews at that time considered Chemosh a real god; it is evident that they believed that every little people had their own god and they would belong to whoever won the day, either the Jewish god or the Moabite god.

Let's provide a third, no less appreciable proof. It is said in the first chapter of Judges (1:19), "Adonai gave them control of the mountains, but they could not conquer the inhabitants of the valleys because they had chariots armed with scythes." We do not want to examine whether the inhabitants of these bristly, mountainous districts, who never had donkeys, could have had war chariots. It is enough to notice that the god of the Jews was at that time only a local god who was respected in the mountains and not at all in the valleys, just like all the other little gods of lands several miles in extent, like Chemosh, Moloch, Rephan, Belphegor, Astaroth, Baal-Berith, Baal-Zebub, and other little grotesqueries.

A fourth proof, stronger than all the others, is taken from the prophets. None of them cites the law of Leviticus or Deuteronomy, but several affirm that the Jews did not worship Adonai in the desert, or that they worshiped other local gods as well. Jeremiah said (49:1), "The lord Moloch has taken the country of Gad." So, there is Moloch considered a god and so well considered a god by the Jews that it is this same Moloch to whom Solomon later sacrificed without any prophet correcting him for it.

Jeremiah also said something even stronger; he made God speak like this (7:22): "When I took your fathers out of Egypt, I did not command them to offer me burnt offerings and sacrifices." Is there anything more precise? Can it be more explicitly stated that the Jews never sacrificed to the God Adonai in the desert?

Amos goes even farther. Here is how he made God speak (5:25–26): "House of Israel, did you offer me sacrifices and offerings for forty years in the desert? You brought the tabernacle of your Moloch, the image of your idols and the star of your God."

We know that all the little peoples of these lands had traveling gods that they put in little chests that we call "arks," for want of a temple. The towns closest to Arabia worshipped stars and put a little figure of a star in their chest.

The opinion that the Jews did not worship Adonai in the desert was so widespread despite Exodus and Leviticus that St. Stephen in his speech to the Sanhedrin did not hesitate to say (Acts 7:43): "You carried the tabernacle of Moloch and the star of your god Rephan who are figures that you made in order to worship them [for forty years]."

You can respond that this adoration of Melchom, Moloch, and Rephan was a betrayal. But an infidelity of forty years and of so many other gods worshipped since then proves well enough that the Jewish religion took a very long time to be formed.

After the death of Gideon it was said (Judges 8:33; 9:4), "The Jews worshipped Baal-Berith." *Baal* is the same thing as *Adonai*; it means "the Lord." The Jews were probably beginning then to learn a little of the Phoenician language and were rendering homage to the Phoenician gods. That is why the worship of Baal lasted such a long time in Israel.

A fifth proof that the Jewish religion was not completely formed is the adventure of Micah recorded in the book of Judges (chap. 17). When a Jewess from the mountain of Ephraim, wife of Micah, had lost 1,100 shekels of silver, an exorbitant sum at that time, one of her sons, who apparently had stolen it, gave it back to her. To thank God for finding her money, this good Jewess set aside two hundred shekels to be thrown into the foundry of idols that it be shut up in a little portable chapel. A Jew of Bethlehem who was a Levite became the priest of this little idolatrous temple, being paid ten shekels a year and his clothes. The good woman then cried out: "God will be good to me because I have a priest of the race of Levi with me."

A few days later six hundred men from the tribe of Dan were going to pillage according to the custom of the Jews, wanting to sack the town of Laish, and they passed by the house of Micah. They met the Levite and asked him if their robbery would be successful. The Levite assured them of their success; they begged him to leave his mistress and be their priest. The chaplain of Micah was won over; then, the tribe of Dan took the priest and the gods and went to kill everyone they came upon in the town of Laish, which was afterward called Dan. The poor woman ran after them screaming and crying. They said to her, "Why are you crying like this?" She answered, "You are carrying away my gods and my priest and everything I have and you ask me why I'm crying." The Vulgate attributes this response to the wife of Micah; but whether she still had a husband or was a widow or the husband or wife cried out, the result is the same that the woman and her husband and their children and Micah's priest and the entire tribe of Dan were idolaters.

What is even more peculiar and more worthy of attention for whoever wants to be educated, is that these same Jews (Judges 18:30) who had sacked the town and country of Dan and stolen the little gods and their brothers, placed these gods in the town of Dan and chose a grandson of Moses with his family to serve them. At least this is what is written in the Vulgate.

It is hard to imagine that the grandson and the entire family of a man who had seen God face to face, who had received the two stone tablets, who had been covered with all the power of God even for forty years, had been reduced to being chaplains of idolatry for a little money. If the first law of the Jews had been at that time to have no carven image, how would the sons of Moses have been suddenly made priests of idols? Therefore, we cannot doubt, based on the very books of the Jews, that their religion was very uncertain, very vague, very weakly established; such, finally, that it should be with a small group of wandering brigands living only off their plunder.

Chapter 17

Continual Change in the Jewish Religion to the Time of the Captivity

When there were only two tribes and some Levites remaining in the house of David, Jeroboam, the chief of the ten other tribes, worshipped different gods than Rohoboam, son of Solomon. This again is at least an irrefutable proof that the Jewish religion was very far from being formed. Rohoboam, for his part, worshipped divinities of whom we had not yet heard. So the Jewish religion, such as it was ordained in the Pentateuch, was entirely neglected. It was said in Kings (2 Kings 16:11) that Ahaz, king of Jerusalem, took the rites of the city of Damascus and had an altar built just like the one in the temple of Damascus. There, certainly, is a religion that is very shaky and very little in tune with itself.

During the reign of Ahaz in Jerusalem, when Hoshea reigned over the ten tribes of Israel, Shalmaneser took this Hoshea into Samaria and put him in chains, chased all ten tribes away from the country and replaced them with people from Babylon, Cuthah and Hamath, and so forth. We hear nothing more about these ten tribes; no one knows today what became of them; they disappeared from the earth before they had their own religion.

But the petty kings of Jerusalem did not long rejoice in the destruction of their brothers. Nebuchadnezzar brought them captive into Babylon with the king of Judah, Jehoiachin, and another king named Zedekiah, whom the conqueror had put in his place. He put out the eyes of Zedekiah, killed his children, burned Jerusalem, knocked down the walls, and brought the whole nation a slave into the states of the king of Babylon.

It is true that all these adventures were recounted in the book of Kings and Chronicles in the most confused and contradictory manner. If you would like to reconcile all the Jewish books, you'd need a volume thicker than the Bible. Let me only mention that these contradictions are a new proof that nothing was clearly established in this nation.

It has been proven, as much as one can prove anything in history, that from the time of their wandering and from the time of their kings the religion of the Jews was only a confused and contradictory hodge-podge of their neighbors' rites. They borrowed the names of God from the Phoenicians; they took the angels from the Persians; they got their wandering ark from the Arabs; they adopted the baptism of the Indians, the circumcision of priests from Egypt, their clothes, their red cow, their cherubim who had a head of a calf and a head of a hawk, their Azazel the scapegoat, and a hundred other ceremonies. Their law (whenever it was written) explicitly forbade them to make any carven image, and their temple was full of them. After their king Solomon consulted the Lord, he placed a dozen figures of calves in the middle of the temple and four-headed cherubim in the sanctuary along with a bronze snake. All this is contradictory, inconsistent, as in almost all nations. It is the nature of man, but the people of God beat all men in this.

The Jews always changed the rites until the time of Esdras and Nehemiah, but they never changed the customs, as they themselves admit. Let's look briefly at what these customs were, after which we shall examine what their religion was when they returned from Babylon.

Chapter 18

Customs of the Jews

We cannot do any better here than to transcribe what Lord Bolingbroke says about the ancient customs of this people in the fifteenth [seventh and eighth] chapter of his *Important Examination*, written in 1736. Maybe it's a little hard, but you have to agree that it's true.

> If we move on from the fables of the Jews to their customs, are they not as abominable as their stories are absurd? They admit that they are a group of brigands who carried into the desert everything they stole from Egypt. Their chief Joshua passed over the Jordan by a miracle like that of the Red Sea. Why? To go to burn and bleed an unknown town, a town whose walls his God brought down at the sound of a trumpet.
>
> The fables of the Greeks were more humane. Amphion built towns with the sound of his flute, Joshua destroyed them; he delivered the elderly, women, children, and animals to fire and sword. Is there a more senseless horror? He only pardoned a prostitute who had betrayed her country. Why did he need the treachery of this unfortunate woman, seeing that his trumpet brought down the walls like Astolfo's and chased everyone away? And I shall mention in passing that this woman, named Rahab the whore, is one of the ancestors of the one we have since made a god, who also counts the

incestuous Tamar, the shameless Ruth, and the adulterous Bathsheba among his forbearers.

They tell us then that this same Joshua conquered thirty-one kings of the country, that is to say thirty-one captains of towns who had fought for their homes against this troupe of assassins. If the author of this history had planned to make the Jews detestable to other nations, would he have gone about it any other way? To add blasphemy to banditry and barbarism, the author dares to say that all these abominations were committed in the name of God, by the express order of God, and were so many sacrifices of human blood offered to God.

That is the holy people! Certainly the Hurons, the Canadians, the Iroquois had philosophers full of humanity compared to the children of Israel; and it is on behalf of these monsters that they make the sun and moon stand still in the middle of the day! And why? To give them time to chase and cut the throats of the poor Amorites, already crushed by a rain of large stones that God had hurled at them from the air above along five long leagues of road. Is this the story of Gargantua? Is this the people of God? And what is more insupportable, the excess of horror or the excess of absurdity? Would it not be another absurdity only to amuse yourself fighting against this detestable heap of fables that equally offends common sense, virtue, nature, and Divinity? If only one of the adventures of these people were unfortunately true, all nations would have united together to exterminate it; if they are false, one cannot tell a more stupid lie.

What shall we say of a Jephthah who immolates his own daughter to his bloodthirsty God, and of the ambidextrous Ehud who assassinates his king Eglon in the name of the Lord, and the divine Jael who murders the general Sisera with a tent peg that she drives into his head, and of the depraved Samson whom God favors with so many miracles?—crude imitations of the fable of Hercules.

Shall we talk about a Levite who came on a donkey with his concubine and with straw and fodder into Gibeah of the tribe of Benjamin? And there are the Benjamites who want to commit the sin of sodomy with this nasty priest like the Sodomites wanted to do with the angels. The Levite capitulates and gives up to them his mistress or his wife whom they enjoy all night long and who is dead the following morning. The Levite cuts up his concubine into a dozen pieces with his knife—which is, however, not an easy thing to do—and from this a civil war ensues.

The eleven tribes arm 400,000 soldiers against the tribe of Benjamin. Four hundred thousand soldiers, good God! In a territory that at the time was not even fifteen leagues long by five or six leagues wide. The Great Turk never had half of such an army. These Israelites exterminate the tribe of Benjamin, the elderly, youth, women, daughters, according to their commendable custom. Six hundred boys escape. One of the tribes cannot perish; they have to give at least six hundred girls to these six hundred boys. What do the Israelites do? There is a little town in the vicinity, named Jabesh—they take it by surprise; kill, massacre everything, even the animals; they set aside four hundred girls for four hundred Benjamites. Two hundred boys remain to take care of; they agree that they will steal two hundred girls of Shiloh when they come out to dance at the gates. Go on Abadie, Sherlock, Houtteville, and friends, tell us something to justify these fables of cannibals, prove that all this is an example, a representation that heralds Jesus Christ.

The Jews have a king in spite of the priest Samuel who does what he can to preserve his usurped authority, and he is bold enough to say that to have a king is to renounce God. In the end, a shepherd looking for donkeys is elected king by lot. The Jews were then under the yoke of the Canaanites—they had never had a temple, their sanctuary was an ark that they put in a cart. The Canaanites had taken their ark. God, though very upset with this, nevertheless let it be taken. But to take vengeance, he had given the conquerors hemorrhoids. The conquerors appeased him by sending back his ark, along with five gold rats and five gold anuses. There is no vengeance or offering more worthy of the God of the Jews. He forgave the Canaanites, but he made 5,070 of them die for looking at his ark.

It is under these lovely circumstances that Saul is elected king of the Jews. There was neither sword nor spear in their small country; the Canaanites and Philistines allowed the Jews, their slaves, to sharpen only their plowshares and their axes; they were forced to go to the Philistine workers for this meager help. And yet, they tell us that King Saul at first had an army of 300,000 with whom he won a great battle. Our Gulliver has similar fables, but none so contradictory.

This Saul, in another battle, comes to terms with the so-called king Agag. The prophet Samuel comes on behalf of the Lord and says to him, "Why haven't you killed everything?" And he takes a holy blade and hacks Agag to pieces. If such an action is true, what a people were these Jews! And what priests!

Saul, reproved by the Lord for not having hacked to pieces his prisoner King Agag, finally goes to fight against the Philistines after the death of the gentle prophet Samuel. He consulted a woman with the spirit of Python about the success of the battle. You know that women with the spirit of Python make shades appear. The pythoness showed Saul the shade of Samuel who came out the earth. But he thinks only of the lovely philosophy of the Jewish people. Now we come to its morality.

A harp player of whom the Eternal was very fond was consecrated king while Samuel was still alive; he revolted against his sovereign, gathered four hundred unfortunates and, as the Holy Scripture says, "All those who were in distress, in debt and discontented gathered around him" (1 Sam. 22:2).

He is a man "after the heart of God" (1 Sam. 16:7) and the first thing he wants to do is to assassinate a landlord called Nabal, who refuses to pay him tribute; he marries eighteen women, not counting concubines; he flees to King Achish, enemy of his country, is well received by him, and in recompense he goes to sack the towns of Achish's allies; he cuts the throats of everyone, not even sparing suckling infants, as the Jewish rite always commands; and he deludes Achish into believing that he sacked Hebrew towns. You have to admit that our highway robbers have been less guilty in the eyes of men, but the ways of the God of the Jews are not ours.

Good King David steals the throne of Ish-Bosheth, son of Saul. He has Mephibosheth killed, the son of his protector Jonathan. He delivers two children of Saul to the Gibeonites along with five of his grandchildren to be hanged. He murders Uriah to cover up his adultery with Bathsheba; and again it is this abominable Bathsheba, mother of Solomon, who is an ancestor of Jesus Christ.

The rest of Jewish history is just a series of petty, holy crimes. Solomon begins by cutting the throat of his brother Adonijah. Though God granted the gift of wisdom to this Solomon, it seems that he refused him the gifts of humanity, justice, continence, and faith. He has seven hundred wives and three hundred concubines. The canticle attributed to him is in the style of those erotic books that make modesty blush. It speaks of sucking breasts, kisses on the mouth and stomach, which is like a mound of wheat, voluptuous positions, a finger put in an opening, quivering and, finally, he ends by saying, "What will we do with our little sister? She doesn't have breasts yet. If she is a wall, let us build on top of it; if she is a door, let us close it" (Canticle 8:8–9). Such are the morals of the wisest of the Jews or at least the morals that the wretched rabbis and the even more absurd Christian theologians reverently ascribe to him.

Of all the kings of Judah and Samaria, there are very few who are not murderers or murdered until finally this motley crew of brigands who massacred one another in public squares and in the temple while Titus was besieging them falls under the sword and into the chains of the Romans and the rest of this little people of God, ten twelfths of whom had been scattered throughout Asia for such a long time, is sold in the markets of Roman cities, every Jewish head being valued at the price of a pig, an animal less impure than this very nation, if what the prophets report is true.

No one can deny that the Jews have written these abominations. When you look at them all together like this, your stomach turns. So these are the heralds of Providence, the precursors of the reign of Jesus!

Chapter 19

The Jewish Religion on the Return from the Captivity in Babylon

Many scholars, after comparing all the texts of the Bible, believed that the Jews had a well-established theology only from the time of Nehemiah after the captivity in Babylon. There were only two tribes and half the Jewish race remaining; their books were lost; the Pentateuch had been unknown for a very long time. It was only found under the king Josiah, twenty-six years before the destruction of Jerusalem and the captivity.

The fourth book of Kings (2 Kings 22:8; 2 Chr. 34:14) says that a high priest named Hilkiah found the book while counting money, gave it to his scribe Shaphan who brought it to the king; the high priest Hilkiah could not very well be bothered to bring the book himself. It concerned the law of the nation, a law written by God himself. You don't send such a book to a sovereign through a clerk along with the receipts and expenses. Scholars have strongly suspected this priest Hilkiah, or Helcias or Helkia, of having compiled the book himself. He could have made some additions, some corrections, although a divine book should never be corrected or added to; but the great Newton thinks that the book had been written by Samuel and he gives rather specious proofs of this. We shall see below on what the scholars have based themselves in assuring us that the Pentateuch could not have been written by Moses.

Be that as it may, almost all men versed in the knowledge of antiquity agree that this book had not been public among the Jews until Esdras and that the Jewish religion did not get a consistent form until that time. They say that even the word *Israel* is convincing enough that the Jews wrote many of their books only during the captivity in Chaldea or immediately afterward. Since the word is Chaldean, this reason does not seem peremptory to me. The Jews very well could have borrowed this word from a neighboring nation a long time beforehand.

But what is more positive and seems to carry more weight is the tremendous number of Persian terms that you find in the Jewish writings. Almost all the names that end in "el" or "al" are either Persian or Chaldean. *Babel*, door of God; *Bathuel*, coming from God; *Phegor-Beel* or *Beel-Phegor*, god of the precipice; *Zebuth-Beel* or *Beel-Zebuth*, god of insects; *Bethel*, house of God; *Daniel*, judgment of God; *Gabriel*, man of God; *Jabel*, afflicted by God; *Jaiel*, the life of God; *Israel*, seeing God; *Oziel*, strength of God; *Raphael*, help of God; *Uriel*, fire of God.

The names and the ministry of angels are obviously taken from the religion of the mages. The word *Satan* is taken from the Persian. The creation of the world in six days is so closely related to the creation the ancient mages said had been made in six gahambars that it seems, in fact, that the Hebrews had taken a great part of their dogma from these same mages, like they got writing when they were slaves in Persia.

What finally persuades some scholars that Esdras completely redid all the Jewish books is that they all exhibit the same style.

What is the result of all these observations? Obscurity and uncertainty.

It is strange that a book written by God himself for the education of the entire world had been unknown for such a long time that there was only one exemplar thirty-six years before the captivity of the two surviving tribes; that Esdras had been forced to reestablish it; that, though made for all nations, it had been absolutely unknown to all nations; and that, though the law it contained was eternal, God himself abolished it.

Chapter 20

The Immortality of the Soul
Is Not Stated or Even Presumed
in Any Place in the Jewish Law

Whoever the author of the Pentateuch was, or rather whoever the writers were who compiled it, whenever it was written, whenever it was published, there is, anyway, the greatest certainty that the system of a future life, of an immortal soul is nowhere found in this book. It is sure that almost all nations surrounding the Jews—Greeks, Chaldeans, Persians, Egyptians, Syrians, and the like— accepted the immortality of the soul and only the Jews had not even examined the question.

We know quite well that neither in Leviticus nor in Deuteronomy did the lawmaker whom they make speak threaten them with any punishment after death or promise them any reward. There were great sects of philosophers everywhere from Peking to Rome who denied the immortality of the soul, but these sects never made laws. No lawmaker proposed that there was only reward and punishment in this life. The lawmaker of the Jews, on the contrary, always said, repeated, inculcated that God would punish human beings only while they were alive. This author, whoever he was, made God himself say, "Honor your father and mother so that you will live a long time" (Ex. 20:12); while the law of the ancient Persians preserved in the Sadder says, "Cherish, serve, comfort your parents so that God will have mercy on you in the other life and your parents will pray for you in the other world" (Art. 13).

"If you obey," says the Jewish lawmaker, "you will have rain in the spring and in the autumn wheat, oil, wine, and hay for your animals," and so forth (Lev. 26:3ff.).

"If you do not keep all the commandments, you will have scabs, pustules, fistula, and ulcers on your knees and in the fat of your legs" [Lev. 26:14ff.].

Above all, he threatens the Jews with being forced to borrow from strangers upon usury and they will be miserable enough not to lend upon usury. He advises them many times to exterminate, massacre all the nations that God delivered them from, to spare neither the elderly, the children, nor the women. But as to the immortality of the soul he never says anything; he never even presumes it.

The philosophers of all countries who denied this immortality gave reasons for it, such as you can see in the third book of Lucretius, but the Jews never gave any reason. If they denied the immortality of the soul, it was solely through crudeness and ignorance; it is because their very crude lawmaker knew no more than they did. When our scholars lately began to read the Jewish books more attentively, they were alarmed to see that in the books attributed to Moses, a future life is never mentioned. They turned themselves every which way trying to find in the Pentateuch what isn't there. They directed themselves to Job as if he had written part of the Pentateuch, but Job was not a Jew. The author of the parable of Job was incontestably an Arab who lived around Chaldea. The Satan that he brings out on the scene with God suffices to prove that the author was not a Jew. The word *Satan* is not found in any of the books of the Pentateuch or even in Judges; it is only in the second book of Kings that the Jews name Satan for the first time (2 Samuel 19:22).

Moreover, it is only in ridiculously interpreting the book of Job that you may try to find some idea of the immortality of the soul in this Chaldean author who wrote long before the Jews had written their Genesis. When Job was overwhelmed with illness, poverty, and even more with the insolent talk of his friends and wife, he said (19:25–26) "that he hopes for recovery, that his skin will return to him, that he will see God in the flesh, that God will be his redeemer, that this redeemer is living, that he will get up one day from the dust on which he is lying." It is clear that this is a sick man who says he will recover. You have to be as absurd as our commentators to see in this speech the immortality of the soul and the coming of Jesus Christ. This insolence would be unimaginable if a hundred other eccentricities didn't carry these gentlemen away.

They have pushed this absurdity so far as to search in passages of Isaiah and Ezekiel for the immortality of the soul that they speak about no more than Job. They distorted a speech of Jacob in Genesis. When the detestable patriarch's children had sold their brother Joseph and came to tell him that he had been devoured by wild beasts, Jacob cried out, "I have nothing left but to die, you will put me in the grave with my son" (Gen. 37:35). This grave, say the Calmets, is hell, so Jacob believed in hell and, consequently, in the immortality of the soul. So, then, poor Calmets, Jacob wanted to go to hell, to be damned because a beast had eaten his son! And of course it was for the patriarchs instead, brothers of Joseph, to be damned; if they believed in hell, the monsters well deserved this punishment.

A well-known author was astonished to see in Deuteronomy a law emanated from God even about the way in which a Jew ought to defecate (23:13) and not to see in all the Pentateuch a single word about human understanding and another life. Whereby this author cried out, "God cares more about their rear end than their soul!" I would not have made this joke. But, certainly, it makes a lot of sense: it is a very strong proof that the Jews only ever thought about their bodies.

Our Warburton wore himself out collecting in his hodgepodge of *Divine Legation* all the proofs that the author of the Pentateuch never spoke of a life to come and it did not bother him much, but he drew an amusing conclusion, worthy of a mind as false as his. He prints in large type, "that the doctrine of a life to come is necessary in every society. All enlightened nations have agreed in the belief and teaching of this doctrine; this wise doctrine has no part in the Mosaic law; therefore, the Mosaic law is divine."

This extreme inconsistency made all England laugh; we tried to outdo each other making fun of him in many writings and he felt the ridicule so strongly that he defended himself only from the crudest injuries.

It is true that in his book he collected many curiosities of antiquity. It is a sewage pit where he throws precious stones taken from the ruins of Greece. We always love to see these ruins, but no one approves of the use that Warburton made to build his antireasonable system.

Chapter 21

That the Jewish Law Is the Only One in the Universe That Ordained Human Sacrifice

The Jews are not only different from other peoples because of their total ignorance of a life to come, but what characterizes them more is that they are also the only ones whose law explicitly ordained the sacrifice of human victims.

The most horrible effect of the superstitions that have flooded the earth is the sacrifice of humans to the Divinity. But this abomination is a lot more natural than you think. The old acts of faith of the Spanish and Portuguese, which, thanks to heaven and to worthy ministers, are no longer repeated; our massacres in Ireland; Saint Bartholomew of France; the popes' crusades against the emperors and then against all the people of Languedoc—were all these dreadful effusions of human blood anything but human sacrifices offered to God by lunatics and barbarians?

In all times they believed they appeased the gods through offerings because they often soothed men's anger by giving them presents, and we have always made God in our image. Nothing is simpler than to offer the blood of our enemies to God. We hate them, so we imagine that our God the protector hates them too. Pope Innocent III, therefore, believed he acted very piously by offering the blood of the Albigensians to Jesus Christ.

It is also simple to offer to our gods what is most precious to us:

and it is even more natural that the priests demanded such sacrifices, given that they always shared with heaven and took the better part. Gold, silver, and jewels are very precious; we always gave them to the priests. What is more precious than our children, especially when they are beautiful? Therefore, on some occasions, in some calamities they have everywhere offered their children to priests for sacrifice and they had to pay the priests the fees for the ceremony. They pushed religious frenzy to the point of sacrificing themselves. But all the time we speak of our bloody and abominable superstitions, don't lose sight of the fact that we must always make an exception of the Chinese, among whom we see no trace of these sacrifices.

Fortunately it is not proven that in antiquity they regularly sacrificed humans on a certain designated day like our Papists do in sacrificing their God every Sunday; we have no law among any people that says on such a day of the month you will sacrifice a girl, on another day a boy. Or even when you have captured a thousand prisoners in battle, you will sacrifice a hundred to your God the protector.

In the *Iliad* Achilles sacrificed twelve young Trojans to the Manes of Patroclus. But he didn't say that this horror was prescribed by law. The Carthaginians, the Egyptians, the Greeks, even the Romans sacrificed humans, but these ceremonies were not established by any law of the country. You do not see in the twelve Roman tables or in the laws of Lycurgus or Solon "that you holily kill girls and boys with a sacred knife." These loathsome devotions seem established only by usage and these hallowed crimes are only very rarely committed.

The Pentateuch is the only ancient monument in which we see a formal law to sacrifice humans, formal commandments to kill in the name of the Lord. Here are these laws:

1. "He who has been offered to Adonai will not be ransomed; he will be put to death" (Lev. 27:29). It is according to this awful law that it was said that Jephthah cut the throat of his own daughter "and he did as he had vowed" (Judges 11:39). After such a clear, affirmative passage, how can we still find hack writers who dare to say that it was about virginity?

2. Adonai says to Moses: "Take vengeance on the Midianites for the sons of Israel. . . . Kill all males, even the children. Cut the throats of all women who have been intimate with men . . . keep for yourselves the virgins. The booty of the army was 675,000 sheep, 72,000

cattle, 61,000 donkeys, and 32,000 virgins who were in the Midianite camp and only two of whom were for Adonai (that is to say, were sacrificed)" and so on (Num. 31:2, 17–18, 32–35). I read in a work called *Proportions* that the number of donkeys was not owing to the number of virgins.

3. It seems that the customs of the Jews was a little bit like the barbarians whom we have found in North America, the Algonquians, Iroquois, and Hurons who carried in triumph the skull and hair of their killed enemies. Deuteronomy 32:42 expressly declares, "I will make my arrows drunk on their blood, my sword will devour the flesh and blood of the dead. They will offer their naked heads to me."

4. Almost all the Jewish canticles that we devotedly recite (and what devotion!) are full of imprecations against all the neighboring peoples. It is only a question of killing, exterminating, disemboweling mothers, and splattering the brains of children on rocks.

5. Adonai pronounces anathema on the king of Arad, the Canaanite prince; the Hebrews kill him and destroy his town (Num. 21).

6. Adonai also expressly says to exterminate all the inhabitants of Canaan: "If you do not want to kill all the inhabitants, I will do to you what I resolved to do to them," that is, I will kill you (Num. 33:56). This law is curious. The author (d'Holbach) of *Christianity Unveiled* says that the souls of Nero, Alexander VI, and his son Borgia all kneaded together could never have imagined anything more abominable.

7. "You will cut the throats of everyone, you will take no compassion on them" (Deut. 7:2).

This here is a small part of the laws given by the mouth of God himself! Gordon, the illustrious author of *Sacerdotal Imposture*, says that if the Jews had known devils as they knew after their captivity in Babylon, they would not have been able to impute to these beings, supposed enemies of the human race, more diabolic commands.

The orders given to Joshua and his successors are no less barbaric. The same author asks what the point is of all these laws that make highway robbers shudder? To make the Jews almost always slaves.

Let's notice here a very important thing. The Jewish God commands his little people to kill everything—the elderly, girls, suckling children, cattle, sheep. Accordingly he promises them the empire of the world. And this little people is enslaved or scattered! Abu Bakr, the second caliph, writes on behalf of God to Yesid, "Kill neither the elderly, women, children, nor animals; cut down no tree." And Abu Bakr was the despot of Asia.

Chapter 22

Reasons of Those Who Claim That Moses Cannot Have Written the Pentateuch

Here are the proofs they offer that if Moses had existed, he could not have written the books attributed to him.

1. It was said that he wrote the Ten Commandments on two tablets of stone. Therefore, he would have also written five huge volumes on stone, which was rather difficult in the desert.

2. It was said that Joshua engraved the Ten Commandments on an altar of uncut stone covered with mortar. This way of writing wasn't done to last forever.

3. Moses could not have said that he was on one side of the Jordan when he was on the other.

4. Moses could not have spoken of towns that did not exist in his time.

5. He could not have given precepts for the conduct of kings when there were no kings.

6. He could not have cited the Book of Jashar, which was written in the time of the kings.

7. He could not have said, when speaking with King Og, that they still saw his iron bed, seeing that this King Og was killed in his time.

8. He could not have commanded his people to pay a half shekel per head, "according to the measure of the temple" (Ex. 30:13; see, my dear reader, if the seal of imposture has ever left a clearer mark),

seeing that the Jews had no temple until many centuries after him. But the great Newton, the learned Leclerc, and many other famous writers have treated this matter so exceptionally that I am embarrassed to even talk about it.

I won't enter into the details here of the dreadful prodigies of which Moses was an eyewitness. Lord Bolingbroke deals very severely with those who attribute the Pentateuch to Moses, and especially with those who make this Moses, at eighty years old, recite a long poem when coming out from the bottom of the Red Sea before three million people when he had to provide for their sustenance.

He says you have to be as idiotic and as cocky as Abadie to dare to offer as proofs of the writing of Moses that he read them to all the Jewish people. This is precisely what is at question. Whoever wrote them six or seven hundred years after him could no doubt say that Moses had read his work to three million Jews gathered together in the desert. This context was no more difficult to imagine than the others. Lord Bolingbroke adds that the puerilities of Abadie and his associates will not support the monstrous structure that crumbles on every side and collapses upon their heads.

A multitude of writers, outraged at all these impostures, still fight against them every day: they demonstrate that there is not one single page of the Bible that isn't faulty or counter to geography; counter to chronology; counter to all the laws of nature, of history; counter to common sense, honor, decency and honesty. Many philosophers, carried away by their zeal, have contemptuously disgraced those who still support these old errors. I do not approve of this bitter zeal: I condemn invectives in a matter that deserves only pity and tears. But I am forced to agree that their reasons deserve the most thoughtful examination. I want only to examine the truth and I disregard the atrocious insults that the two sides have vomited against each other for so long.

Chapter 23

If Moses Existed

We have among us a quite famous sect called Freethinkers, much more widespread than the Freemasons. I consider the main heads of this sect Lord Herbert; Sirs Raleigh and Sydney; Lord Shaftesbury; the wise Locke, moderate to the point of timidity; the great Newton, who so boldly denied the divinity of Jesus Christ; Collins; Toland; Tindale; Trenchard; Gordon, Woolston; Wollaston; and above all the famous Lord Bolingbroke. Many of them have pushed the spirit of examination and critique to the point of doubting the existence of Moses. We must impartially deduce the reasons for these doubts.

If Moses was a character like Solomon, to whom they attribute only some books that he didn't write, some treasures that he didn't possess, and a palace far too luxurious for a little king of Judea, we would not have the right to deny the existence of such a man, for one can very well not be the author of the Canticle of Canticles, not possess a billion pounds sterling in the coffers, not have seven hundred wives and three hundred concubines, and yet be a very well-known king.

Flavius Josephus informs us that the contemporary Tyrian authors mentioned Solomon in the archives of Tyre. There is nothing offensive to reason here. Neither the birth of Solomon, son of double adultery, nor his death has anything wondrous that is shocking to nature or inspires disbelief.

But if everything in the life of a man is like a fantastic novel, from his birth to his death, then it is necessary to have proofs that are as clear as day; it is necessary to have the most irreproachable contemporary witnesses. It is not enough for a priest, a thousand years later, to have found a book about this man in a trunk while he was counting some money and to have sent it with his scribe to a petty king.

If today a Russian bishop sent from the depths of Tartary to the empress a book composed by the Scythian Abaris, which he had found in a sacristy or in an old trunk, it is not likely that this princess would put much faith in such a work. The author of this book would have to ensure that Abaris had run around the world riding an arrow, that this arrow was precisely the one Apollo used to kill the Cyclops, that Abaris hid this arrow near Moscow, that the winds had offered it to the Tartar Abaris, great poet and sorcerer, who made a talisman with the bones of Pelops. It is certain that the court of Petersburg would not believe anything at all today, but the people of Kazan and Astrakhan could have believed it two or three centuries ago.

The same thing would happen with the king of Denmark and his entire court if you brought him a book written by the god Odin. You would be meticulously questioned whether any German or Swedish writers knew this Odin and his family and whether they spoke about him honestly.

Moreover, if his contemporaries spoke only about the miracles of Odin, if Odin never did anything that wasn't supernatural, he would run the risk of being discredited at the court of Denmark. We wouldn't think any different about him than we do of the wizard Merlin.

Moses seems to be precisely in this situation in the eyes of those who submit to the evidence. No Egyptian or Phoenician writer speaks about Moses in ancient times. The Chaldean Berossus says not a word: for, if he had mentioned him, the church fathers (as I already mentioned concerning Sanchuniathon) would have all gloated over this evidence. Flavius Josephus, who wanted to valorize this Moses (though he doubts all his miracles), searched everywhere for some evidence concerning the deeds of Moses but found nothing. He dared not say that Berossus, born under the reign of Alexander, reported even one single deed attributed to Moses.

Finally, he found a Cheremon of Alexandria, who lived in the time of Augustus around 1,500 or 1,600 years after the epoch in which we place Moses; this writer said nothing about Moses except that he was chased out of Egypt.

He went to consult the book of another older Egyptian named Manetho. He lived under the reign of Ptolemy Philadelphus, three hundred years before our era, and already the Egyptians had abandoned their barbaric tongue for the beautiful Greek language. Manetho wrote in Greek; he wrote nearer to Moses than Cheremon by more than three hundred years; Josephus fared no better with him. Manetho said that there was once a priest of Heliopolis named Osarsiph who took the name Moses and fled with some lepers.

It could very well be that the Jews spoke for so long about their Moses to their neighbors that word finally got around to some writers in Egypt; and from there to the Greeks and Romans. Strabo, Diodorus, and Tacitus have only a few words to say about him; even these are vague, very confused, and opposed to everything the Jews wrote. This here is not evidence. If some French writer dared to mention our Merlin today, this would not prove that Merlin spent his life performing prodigies.

Every nation wanted to have its illustrious founders and lawmakers. Our neighbors the French imagined a Francus whom they called the son of Hector. The Swedes are very sure that Magog, son of Japheth, gave them laws immediately after the flood. Another son of Japheth named Tubal was the lawmaker of Spain. Josephus called him Thobel, which should heighten our respect for this Jewish historian.

All the nations of antiquity fabricated even more extravagant origins. This passion to surpass one's neighbors in chimeras went so far that the people of Mesopotamia bragged about having had for their lawmaker the fish Oannes, which left the Euphrates twice a day to preach to them.

Moses could very well be a lawmaker as imaginary as this fish. A man who changes his rod into a snake and a snake into a rod, who crosses the sea with dry feet along with three million people, a man finally in the so-called writings in which a donkey speaks is no better than a talking fish.

These here are the reasons on which doubts of the existence of Moses are based. But the response seems, perhaps, to be as strong as the objections: that the enemies of the Jews have never doubted it.

Chapter 24

On a Very Curious Life of Moses Written by the Jews after the Captivity

T he Jews have such a passion for the imaginary that when their conquerors allowed them to return to Jerusalem, they decided to compose a history of Moses even more fantastic than what had been called canonical. We have a quite considerable fragment of it translated by the learned Gilbert Gaulmin, dedicated to Cardinal Bérulle. Here are the main adventures reported in this fragment as peculiar as it is little known.

One hundred and thirty years after the establishment of the Jews in Egypt and sixty years after the death of the patriarch Joseph, the pharaoh had a dream in his sleep. An old man was holding a balance; in one of the pans were the inhabitants of Egypt, in the other was a young child and this child weighed more than all the Egyptians put together. The pharaoh straightway called his *shotim*, his sages. One of them told him, "O king! This child is a Jew who will one day do great harm to your kingdom. Kill all the children of the Jews; thus you will save your empire, if, however, you can stand in the way of destiny."

This advice pleased the pharaoh. He summoned the midwives and ordered them to strangle all the males to whom the Jews gave birth. . . . There was in Egypt a man named Abraham or Amram, son of Kohath, married to Jochebed, sister of his brother. Jochebed gave him a daughter called Mariam, which means "persecuted," because the

Egyptian descendants of Ham persecuted the Israelites. Jochebed then gave birth to Aaron, which means "condemned to death," because the pharaoh had condemned all the Jewish children to death. Aaron and Mariam were saved by the angels of the Lord who fed them in the fields and brought them to their parents when they were adolescents.

Finally Jochebed had a third child: this was Moses (who, as a result, was fifteen years younger than his brother). He was set upon the Nile. The pharaoh's daughter found him while she was bathing, fed him, and adopted him as her son, although she was not married.

Three years later her father the pharaoh got a new wife. He had a grand feast; his wife was on his right, his daughter on his left with little Moses. As the child was playing, he took the crown and put it on his head. Then Balaam the magician, the king's eunuch, remembered His Majesty's dream. "There," he said, "is the child who one day will do so much harm; the spirit of God is in him. What he just did is a proof that he already has definite plans to dethrone you. You have to destroy him right away." The pharaoh was very pleased with this idea.

They were going to kill little Moses when God right away sent his angel Gabriel, dressed up like an official of the pharaoh, and he said, "Lord, you cannot kill an innocent infant who has not yet reached the age of discretion; he only put your crown on his head because he lacks prudence. You just have to offer him a ruby and a red hot coal; if he chooses the coal, he is clearly an imbecile who will not be dangerous; but if he takes the ruby, it is a sign that he understands delicacy and then you must kill him."

They immediately brought a ruby and coal. Moses did not fail to take the ruby, but the angel Gabriel, by slight of hand, slipped the coal in place of the precious stone. Moses put the coal into his mouth and burned his tongue so horribly that he stammered the rest of his life. And that is the reason why the lawmaker of the Jews could not speak clearly.

Moses was fifteen years old and was the pharaoh's favorite. A Hebrew man came to complain to him that an Egyptian had beaten him up after sleeping with his wife. Moses killed the Egyptian. The pharaoh ordered them to cut off the head of Moses. The executioner struck him, but God right away changed the neck of Moses into a column of marble and sent the angel Michael who in three days' time led Moses beyond the borders.

The young Hebrew took refuge with Mecano, king of Ethiopia, who was at war with the Arabs. Mecano made him general of his army, and after Mecano's death Moses was elected king and married the widow. But Moses, ashamed to be married to the wife of his lord, did not dare enjoy her and put a sword in the bed between him and the queen. He stayed with her forty years without touching her. The angered queen finally summoned the states of the kingdom of Ethiopia, complained that Moses was doing nothing with her, and decided to chase him away and put the son of the late king on the throne.

Moses fled to the land of Midian to the priest Jethro. This priest believed that his fortune would be made if he delivered Moses into the hands of the pharaoh of Egypt and so he put him in the bottom of a pit where he gave him only bread and water. Moses grew visibly fat in his dungeon. Jethro was utterly astonished. He did not know that his daughter Zipporah was falling in love with the prisoner and bringing him partridges and quail with good wine. He figured that God was protecting Moses, and he did not deliver him to the pharaoh.

Meanwhile, good old Jethro wanted to marry off his daughter. He had a sapphire tree on which was engraved the name of Jaho or Jehovah. He announced throughout the land that he would give his daughter to whomever could uproot the sapphire tree. Zipporah's lovers showed up, but none of them could even bend the tree. Moses, who was only seventy-seven years old, suddenly uprooted the tree with no problem. He married Zipporah, with whom he soon had a beautiful boy named Gershom.

One day while walking Moses met God in a bush, who ordered him to go and perform miracles at the palace of the pharaoh: he left with his wife and son. On the way they met an unnamed angel who ordered Zipporah to circumcise the young Gershom with a stone knife. God sent Aaron on the road, but Aaron thought it very bad that his brother had married a Midianite; he treated her like a whore and young Gershom like a bastard, and sent them back to their country by the shortest route.

Then Aaron and Moses went alone into the palace of the pharaoh. The palace door was guarded by two enormously large lions. Balaam, the king's magician, saw the two brothers coming and loosed upon them the two lions, but Moses touched them with his rod and the two lions humbly prostrated themselves, licking the feet of Aaron and

Moses. The king, utterly astonished, had the two pilgrims brought before all his magicians, to see who could perform the most miracles.

The author recounts here the ten plagues of Egypt pretty much as they are told in Exodus. He adds only that Moses buried all of Egypt elbow-deep in lice and sent among all the Egyptians lions, wolves, bears, and tigers that entered the houses, even though the doors were locked, and ate all the young children.

According to this author, it was not the Jews who fled by the Red Sea; it was the pharaoh who fled by this route with his army. The Jews ran after them, the waters parted to the left and right to see them fight; all the Egyptians, except for the king, were killed on the sand. So when this king saw that he was up against a strong opponent, he asked forgiveness of God. Michael and Gabriel were sent to him; they transported him to the town of Nineveh where he reigned for four hundred years.

If we compare this story with that of Exodus and have to chose one over the other, for my part I am not learned enough to judge. I only agree that both are imaginary fiction.

Chapter 25

On the Death of Moses

Besides this life of Moses, we have two no less admirable accounts of his death. The first is in a long conversation Moses had with God in which God announced to him that he had no more than three hours to live. The bad angel Samael was present at the conversation. When the first hour had passed, he started to laugh because he was soon going to take hold of Moses' soul; and Michael started to cry. "Don't rejoice so much, wicked beast," said the good angel to the bad. "Moses is going to die, but we have Joshua in his place."

When the three hours had passed, God commanded Gabriel to take the soul of the dying man. Gabriel excused himself, Michael too. Refused by the two angels, God addressed Zinguiel. He no more wanted to obey than the others. "It is me," he said, "who was once his tutor; I won't kill my student." Then God became angry and said to the bad angel Samael, "Well then, wicked one, take his soul." Full of joy, Samael took his sword and ran to Moses. The dying man rose up in anger, his eyes glaring. "Scoundrel," Moses said to him, "how dare you kill me, I who put the pharaoh's crown on my head as an infant, I who performed miracles at the age of eighty, I who led sixty million people out of Egypt, I who split the Red Sea in two, I who conquered two kings who were so big that at flood times the water only came up to their knees? Go on, rascal, get out of my face right now."

This altercation lasted a few moments. During this time Gabriel prepared a stretcher to transport the soul of Moses, Michael a purple coat, Zinguiel a robe. God put his two hands on his chest and took away his soul.

It is to this story that the apostle Saint Jude makes allusion in his Epistle when he says that the archangel Michael fought with the devil over the body of Moses. Since this deed is found only in the book I have just cited, it is evident that Saint Jude had read it and that he considered it canonical.

The second story of the death of Moses is also a conversation with God. It is just as amusing and curious as the first. Here are some lines of dialogue:

> Moses: I beg you, Lord, let me enter the Promised Land, at least for three or four years.
> God: No, I have decreed that you will not enter there.
> Moses: Then, at least carry me there after my death.
> God: No, neither living nor dead.
> Moses: Alas! Good God, you are so merciful toward your creatures, you forgive them two or three times, I have committed only one sin and you do not forgive me!
> God: You know not what you say; you have committed six sins. . . . I remember having sworn either your death or the loss of Israel; one of these two oaths has to be accomplished. If you want to live, Israel will perish.
> Moses: Lord, that is too cunning; you are holding the rope at both ends. Let Moses perish rather than a single soul of Israel.

After several speeches like this the echo of the mountain said to Moses, "You have no more than five hours to live." At the end of five hours, God sent Gabriel, Zinguiel, and Samael to get him. God promised Moses to bury him and carry away his soul.

All these stories are no more extraordinary than is the history of Moses in the Pentateuch. It is up to the reader to judge.

Chapter 26

If the History of Bacchus
Is Taken from That of Moses

I have already mentioned an amazing resemblance between what antiquity says about Moses and what it says about Bacchus. They have the same name, lived in the same country, performed the same miracles, wrote their laws on stone; which of the two is the original? Which is the copy? What is certain is that Bacchus was known to almost every land before any nation, except the Jewish, had ever heard of Moses. No Greek writer spoke of the writings that they attribute to this Jew before the rhetorician Longinus who lived in the third century of our era. The Greeks did not even know if the Jews had books. The historian Josephus confessed in the fourth chapter of his *Against Apion* that the Jews had no commerce with other peoples. "The country we live in," he said, "is far from the sea; we do not have commerce, we do not communicate with other peoples." And then: "Therefore, is it any wonder that, since our nation is so far from the sea and pretends to have written nothing, it has been so little known?"

Nothing is more affirmative than this passage. The mysteries of Bacchus were already celebrated in Greece; Asia knew them before any people had heard of the Hebrew Moses. It is very natural that a little, barbaric, unknown nation imitate a great, civilized, illustrious nation; there are so many examples that this thought alone is enough to make the Jews lose their case. In the matter of fables like in all inventions, it seems that the more ancient served as models for others. *The Golden Legend* is full of all the fables of ancient Greece with Christian names. You find there the complete story of Hippolytus and Oedipus. There is a saint to whom a stag predicts that he will kill his father and sleep with his mother. The stag's prediction comes true; the saint repents and is in the martyrology. People love fables so much that when they cannot invent them, they copy them.

I have made these comments so that you might guard against the fictional spirit of antiquity that has been perpetuated for too long.

Chapter 27

On the Cosmogony Attributed to Moses and the Flood

Since the whole Jewish religion was based on the creation of man, on the formation of woman from Adam's rib, on the express orders of God given to this Adam and his wife, on the transgression of these two first creatures deceived by a snake who spoke and walked on feet, and so forth, since Moses learned all these things from the mouth of God himself, since he wrote in the name of God as an eternal monument for the human race, how could it have been forbidden to the Jews to read Genesis before the age of twenty-five? Was it because the Sanhedrin were afraid that at eighteen or twenty they would make fun of it? If the reading of Genesis were scandalous, the older you are, the more scandalous it should have been. If you respect the lawmaker, why forbid reading his law?

If God is the father of all people, why were their creation and initial actions, written by God himself, not known by all people? Why was Moses the only one instructed at the end of 2,500 years in a desert?

How is it, for example, that in the time of Augustus, there was not a single historian, a single poet, a single scholar who knew the names Adam, Eve, Abel, Cain, Methuselah, Noah, and the like? Every nation has its cosmogony. There isn't a single one that resembles the Jewish one. Certainly the Indians, Scythians, Persians, Egyptians, Greeks, and Romans do not count their years starting from Adam or Noah or Abraham. It must be admitted that the Varros and Plinys would die laughing if they could see our almanacs today, "Abel died in the year 130. Death of Adam in the year 930. Universal Flood in 1656 . . . Noah leaves the ark in 1657. . . ." This astonishing usage to which we all bow our heads is not even noticed. These calculations are at the beginning of all the almanacs of Europe, and no one considers that all this is still unknown to the rest of the earth.

Let's suppose that Sanchuniathon had written at the same time as we place Moses (though he certainly wrote long before)—how can it be that Sanchuniathon did not speak about Adam, Noah, or the universal flood? Why was this prodigious event, which reduced the entire earth to a single family, totally unknown in all antiquity? There were floods, no doubt; countries were submerged by the sea. The floods of Deucalion and Ogyges were quite well known. Plato said that the island of Atlantis was once submerged. Whether fable or truth, it doesn't matter; no one ever doubted that many parts of the globe suffered great revolutions, but the universal deluge such as they recount is physically impossible. Neither Thucydides nor Herodotus nor any other ancient historian dishonored his pen by such a fable.

If there had been some remembrance of so strange an event among men, would Hesiod or Homer have passed over it in silence? Would there not be found some allusions in the poets, some comparisons drawn from this upheaval of nature? Would there not be some verse of Orpheus preserved in which we could find some traces?

The Jews could not have imagined a universal flood except after having heard about some particular flood. Since they had no knowledge of the globe, they took a part for the whole, the inundation of a small country for the inundation of the entire earth. They exaggerated; and what people were not exaggerators?

Some storytellers, some poets later exaggerated among the Greeks, and from the flood of a part of Greece they made a universal flood. Ovid celebrated it in his charming book *Metamorphoses*. He was right: such an affair is made only for poetry. For us it is a miracle; for the Greeks and Romans it was a fable.

There were still other floods than in Greece, and they were probably the source of the narrative of the flood that the Jews made in their Genesis when they wrote it later under the name of Moses.

Eusebius and George Syncellus, that is, the chronicler, have preserved for us fragments of a certain Abydenus. This Abydenus had transcribed some fragments of Berossus, an ancient Chaldean writer. This Berossus wrote stories and in these stories he spoke about a flood that occurred under the king of Chaldea named Xissuther, since then called Xisouthros, who they suppose had lived in the time when Noah lived.

So, this Berossus said that a Chaldean god, since then recognized as Saturn, appeared to Xissuther and told him, "On the fifteenth of the month of Daesius the human race will be destroyed by a flood. Lock up tightly all your writings in Sippara, the city of the sun, so that the memory of things not be lost (for when no one is left on the earth, the writings will be very necessary). Build a vessel, go into it with your family and friends, bring in birds and quadrupeds, put there provisions, and when they ask you where you want to go with your vessel, answer: Toward the gods to beg them to favor the human race."

Xissuther did not fail to build his vessel, which was two stadia wide and five long, that is, its width was 250 geometrical feet and its length was 625. This vessel that should have gone on the Black Sea was a poor sailboat. The flood came. When the flood had stopped, Xissuther released some of the birds that returned to the vessel after finding nothing to eat. A few days later he again released some birds that returned with mud on their feet. Finally, they did not return. Xissuther did the same: he left his vessel, which was perched on a mountain in Armenia, and returned no more; the gods lifted him up.

That is the only basis of the now so popular fable that Noah's ark came to rest on a mountain in Armenia and that we can still see its remains.

Perhaps some readers may think that the story of Noah is a copy of the fable of Xissuther. They will say that if lesser peoples always copy the great, if the Chaldeans and all the neighboring peoples were unquestionably more ancient than the Jews, if the Jews were, in fact, so recent, it is also probable that they imitated their neighbors in everything except for the sciences and arts that this crude people could never attain. For me again, I content myself with respecting the Bible.

The skeptics allege that it is very likely that the Pontos Euxeinos (the Black Sea) once broke its boundaries and flooded part of ancient Armenia. The Aegean Sea could have done the same in Greece; the Atlantic Sea could have swallowed up a great island. The Jews, who would have vaguely heard about this, would have adapted the event and invented Noah. It is incontestable, they add, that there was never a Noah; for, if such a character had existed, he would have been considered by all nations a restorer and the father of the human race. It would have been impossible to lose the memory. Noah would have been the first word that the entire human race pronounced. This Jewish fable was, as has already been said, entirely unknown to the entire world until the time when the Christians began to introduce the Jewish books through Greek translations. Finally, seeing that the Jews were only plagiarizers about all the rest, they could well have been so about the Flood. I am only reporting the arguments of the Freethinkers, to which the Nonthinkers respond with the authenticity of the Pentateuch.

Chapter 28

On the Plagiarisms
Blamed on the Jews

1. Sanchuniathon, who wrote long before the Jews were gathered together in the desert, gave ten generations of men up to the time of the so-called universal flood. The books attributed to Moses also supposed ten generations.

2. The curiosity of a woman named Pandora was fatal to the human race. The curiosity of a woman named Eve got the human race chased from the so-called paradise.

3. Bacchus gave a law written on two marble tablets, raised the waters of the Red Sea to the right and left to permit his army to go through, and held the sun and moon in their course. Moses also gave laws written on two stone tablets, crossed the Red Sea with dry feet, and his successor Joshua stopped the sun and moon.

4. Minerva made a fountain of oil spring forth, Bacchus a fountain of wine. Moses gave to the Jews only a fountain of water in the desert.

5. Philemon and Baucis welcomed two gods in Phrygia whom a town around Tyana had refused; the gods changed their house into a temple and the town into a lake. The Jews imitated this fable in the most infamous manner, saying that the inhabitants of the town of Sodom wanted to rape two angels. And Sodom was changed into a lake.

6. The Greeks supposed that Agamemnon wanted to sacrifice his daughter Iphigenia and that the gods sent a doe to be sacrificed in her place. The Jews supposed that Abraham wanted to sacrifice his son and that Adonai sent a ram to be sacrificed in place of Isaac.
7. Niobe was changed into a statue of marble. Edith, the wife of Lot, was changed into a statue of salt.
8. Labors of Hercules. Labors of Samson.
9. Hercules betrayed by woman. Samson betrayed by woman.
10. The ass of Silenus talks. The ass of Balaam talks.
11. Hercules lifted into the heavens in a chariot. Elijah rises into the heavens in a chariot.
12. The gods resurrect Pelops. Elisha resurrects a young girl.

If you would like to take pains to compare all the events of fable and ancient Greek history, you would be astonished to find not a single page of the Jewish books that wasn't plagiarized.

Finally, the verses of Homer were already sung in more than two hundred cities before these two hundred cities knew that the Jews existed in the world. Reader, examine and judge. Decide between those whom we call Freethinkers and those whom we call Nonthinkers.

Chapter 29

On the Worship of the Jews and Their Conduct after the Captivity up to the Reign of the Idumean Herod

It is peculiar to the Jews to be brokers, retailers, and usurers everywhere; to amass money by frugality and thrift. Money was the object of their conduct at all times to the point that in the story of their Tobit (canonical book or not) an angel descends from heaven during their captivity not to console the scattered unfortunates, not to bring them to Jerusalem (which an angel could have undoubtedly done), but to lead the young Tobit into a town in Media to ask for money back that was owed to his father.

> Let others melt with softer mold the breathing bronze, etc.
> You, *Jews*, be mindful to *squeeze* the people with *usury*.
> (Cf. Virgil, *Aeneid*, 6.847 and 851)

So, they were traders for the seventy-two years of their migration. They earned a lot and since they always paid and still do in many states, even in Rome, to get the permission to have synagogues, it is most likely that they gave a lot of money to the treasury commissioners of Cyrus and to the finance minister to permit them to rebuild their city with a little temple, half in stone and half in wood. But when they returned to their Jerusalem or Hershalaim, they were hardly more fortunate.

Subjects or rather slaves of the Persian kings, then of Alexander, sometimes of the kings of Syria, sometimes of Egypt, they no longer made up a state. They were very much like the province of Gaul compared to England at the time of Henry VIII. The interior of their little republic was no longer administered by anyone but priests. At that time everything was fixed and determined in their sect; they were more devout than ever. They were so much more Jewish that the Samaritans despised being so and being considered their compatriots. These Samaritans did not want to have anything in common with the Jewish people, not even their God. The historian Josephus (*Jewish Antiquities*, XII, 5) mentions that they wrote to the king of Syria, Antiochus Epiphanes, that "their temple bore the name of no god," that they did not take part in the Judaic superstitions, and that they were supplicating him to allow them to dedicate their temple to Jupiter.

When Antiochus Epiphanes had some pigs sacrificed in the temple of Jerusalem, some sensible Jews said nothing. But most of them believed it was an abominable impiety. They thought that God did not love pig flesh, that he absolutely needed lambs or goats, and that it was a horrible sin to sacrifice pork. The Maccabees took advantage of these fine prejudices of the people to revolt. This revolt that the Jews have praised so highly and that all our preachers offer so often as a model did not prevent Antiochus Eupator, son of Epiphanes, from demolishing the walls of the temple and cutting off the head of the high priest Onias, who instigated the rebellion.

The Jews, for whom God had performed so many miracles, who according to the oracles of their prophets should have ruled the entire world, were then even more unfortunate, more humiliated under the Seleucids than under the Persians and Babylonians.

After countless revolutions and miseries, citizens rose up among them who robbed the priests of their usurped authority and took the name of king. These so-called kings were no better than the pontiffs; they cut one another's throats just like they did before the Babylonian captivity.

Just in passing, Pompey put one of these kings named Aristobulus in prison and then hanged his son, the little king Alexander.

Some time after the Triumvirate, Mark Antony gave the kingdom of Judea to the Idumean Arab Herod. He is the only Jewish king who was truly powerful. He was the one who built a magnificent temple on a large platform connected to the mountain Moriah by bridging a canyon. The temple of Solomon built on the side of the mountain could only have been a clumsy and barbaric building in which it was necessary to climb up and down constantly.

Herod, after having repressed many revolts, was absolute master under the protection of the Romans.

Chapter 30
On the Customs of the Jews under Herod

The Jewish people were so strange, they lived in such anarchy, they were so devoted to robbery before the reign of Herod that they treated this prince as a tyrant when he ordained by a very reasonable law that they would thereafter sell outside the kingdom anyone who robbed houses after having breached the walls; they complained that he was taking away from them the most precious of their freedoms. Above all they considered this law a manifest impiety. "How dare they sell," they said, "a Jewish thief to a foreigner who was not of the holy religion?" This fact, reported in Josephus (*Jewish Antiquities*, XVI, 1), perfectly characterizes the people of God.

Herod reigned for thirty-five years with some glory. He was indisputably the richest and most powerful of all the Jewish kings, including David and Solomon despite their so-called treasury of around one billion of our pounds sterling.

Since under his reign Judea was not infested with foreign invasions, the Jews had time to turn their minds toward controversy. This is what occupies all superstitious and ignorant people today when they have no public games or entertainment: they give themselves over to theological disputes. This is what happened under the deplorable reign of our Charles I and what clearly shows that it is always necessary to feed people's idleness with entertainment.

The Pharisees and the Sadducees troubled the state as much as they could, like the Episcopalians and Presbyterians do among us. John the Baptist passed himself off as a prophet; he administered the ancient Jewish baptism and had a following among the people. The historian Josephus (XVIII, 5) explicitly said that he was a good man who exhorted the people to virtue, but Herod, fearing sedition because the people gathered around John, had him imprisoned in the fortress of Macherus, like they say the Jansenists are imprisoned in France.

Above all, notice here that Josephus does not say that they then killed John under the government of Herod the Tetrarch. No one should have been better informed of this fact than Josephus, a contemporary writer, an accredited writer, of the race of Asmoneans and vested with public offices.

They argued about the Messiah, the Christ, in the time of Herod. He was a liberator that the Jews waited for in all their afflictions, especially under the kings of Syria. They had given this name to Judas Maccabee; they had given it to Cyrus and some other foreign princes. Many took Herod as a Messiah; there was a formal sect of Herodians. Others, who considered his government tyrannical, called him the anti-Messiah, anti-Christ.

Some time after his death there was a maniac called Theudas who passed for the Messiah. Josephus (XX, 2) said that he was followed by a great multitude of riffraff to whom he promised to make the Jordan roll back to its source like Joshua did and that everyone who wanted to follow him would cross with dry feet. He left them to have his head cut off.

The whole Jewish nation was fanatical. The devout ran around proselytizing, baptizing, circumcising. There were two kinds of baptism, one of the proselyte and the other of justice. Those who were converted to Judaism and lived among the Jews without claiming to be part of the nation were not forced to receive baptism or circumcision. They were almost always content to be baptized. This is less painful than having their foreskin cut; but those who had a higher calling and were called proselytes of justice received both signs: they were baptized and circumcised. Josephus (XX, 2) relates that there was a minor king of the province of Adiabene, called Izates, who was stupid enough to embrace the religion of the Jews. He did not say where this province of Adiabene was, but there was one around the Euphrates. They baptized and circumcised Izates; his mother Helena was content to be baptized with the baptism of justice and they cut nothing off her.

In the midst of all these Jewish factions, all the eccentric superstitions and their plundering spirit, we see, as elsewhere, virtuous men just like in Rome and in Greece. There were even groups that in a way resembled the Pythagoreans and Stoics. They respected temperance, the spirit of retreat, strict manners, distance from all pleasures, and a taste for the contemplative life. Such were the Essenes; such were the Therpeutae.

You should not be surprised that under as vicious a prince as Herod and under the former kings even more vicious than he, you could see such virtuous men. Epictetus was in Rome in the time of Nero. Some even believed that Jesus Christ was an Essene, but it is not true. The Essenes held it a principle to not put on a show, to not attract a following, to not speak in public. They were virtuous for themselves and not for others. They did not flaunt it. Everyone who wrote the life of Jesus Christ characterized him as the complete opposite and much superior.

Chapter 31

On Jesus

Only a fanatic or stupid rogue could say that you should never examine the story of Jesus with the lights of reason. With what will you judge a book, whatever it may be? Is it with folly? I put myself here in the place of a citizen of ancient Rome who was reading the stories of Jesus for the first time.

We have Hebrew and Greek books for and against Jesus that are equally old—the *Toledat Yeshu* and the *Toledat Jesu* writings against him in Hebrew. In these books they treat him as a bastard, an impostor, an insolent, seditious wizard; and in the Greek Gospels they make him almost a participant in divinity itself. All these writings are full of prodigies and at first seem to our feeble eyes to contain contradictions on almost every page.

An illustrious writer who was born very soon after the death of Jesus and who, if you believe St. Irenaeus (who asserts that Jesus died at the age of fifty; in this case, Flavius Josephus could well have seen him), should have been his contemporary; in short, Flavius Josephus, close friend of the wife of Herod, son of a sacrificing priest, who should have known Jesus, does not have the shortcoming of those who speak about him so abusively and is not of the opinion of those who praise him so profusely. He says nothing at all. It is proven today that the five or six lines about Jesus attributed to Josephus were interpolated by a very awkward fraud. For, if Josephus had in fact believed Jesus was the Messiah, he would have written a hundred times more; and in acknowledging him as the Messiah he would have been one of his followers.

Justus of Tiberias, another Jew who wrote the history of his country a little before Josephus, keeps deadly silent about Jesus. It is Photius who assures us of this.

Philo, another famous Jewish writer of the time, never cited the name of Jesus. No Roman historian speaks of the prodigies that are attributed to him and that should have made the land heedful.

Let us also add an important truth to these historical truths, which is that neither Josephus nor Philo made the least mention in any place about the expectation of a Messiah.

Will you conclude from this that there was no Jesus, just like some have dared to conclude from the Pentateuch itself that there was no Moses? No, seeing that after the death of Jesus they wrote for and against him, it is clear that he existed. It is no less evident that he was then so hidden from people that no citizen, even a little eminent in the world, made mention of his person.

I saw some disciples of Bolingbroke, more ingenious than educated, who denied the existence of Jesus because the story of the three wise men and the star and the massacre of the innocents are, they said, the height of eccentricity; the contradiction of the two genealogies that Matthew and Luke gave is especially a reason that these young men allege to persuade themselves that there was no Jesus. But they drew a very false conclusion.

Our compatriot Howell had a very ridiculous genealogy made in France; some Irishmen wrote that he and Jansen had familiar spirits who always gave them aces when they were playing cards. They made up a hundred crazy stories about them. This does not prevent them from really existing; whoever lost their money to them was well convinced of this.

What foolish things have not been said of the Duke of Buckingham? He nonetheless lived under James and Charles.

Apollonius of Tyana certainly resurrected no one; Pythagoras did not have a golden thigh. But Apollonius and Pythagoras were real beings. Maybe our divine Jesus was not really taken up onto a mountain by the devil. He did not really dry up a fig tree in March because it bore no figs, *even though it was not the time for figs.* Maybe he did not descend into hell, and so on. But there was a Jesus to be respected only by consulting reason.

Who was this man? The two sides agree that he was the son of a village carpenter; they argue about his mother. The enemies of Jesus say that she was impregnated by a man called Panther. His partisans say that she became pregnant by the spirit of God. There is no middle ground between the two opinions of the Jews and Christians. The Jews, however, were able to accept a third sentiment that is more natural, which is that her husband, who gave her other children, gave her this one also; but the partisan spirit is never moderate. The result of this diversity of opinions is that Jesus was born an unknown among the dregs of society; and it turns out that being given to prophesize like so many others and having never written anything, the pagans were able to reasonably doubt that he knew how to write, which would be appropriate to his status and education.

But humanly speaking, could a supposedly ignorant carpenter from Nazareth have founded a sect? Yes, like our Fox, a very ignorant village cobbler, founded the sect of Quakers in the county of Leicester. He ran around the fields dressed in a leather outfit; he was a madman with a strong imagination who spoke with enthusiasm to weak imaginations. Having read the Bible, applying it in his way, he gathered a following of imbeciles; he was ignorant, but learned men succeeded him. The sect of Fox took form and survived honorably after having been jeered at and persecuted. The first Anabaptists were hapless, unlettered peasants.

Finally, the example of Mohammed is irrefutable. He was given the title of ignorant prophet. Many people even doubt that he knew how to write. The fact is that he wrote badly and fought well. He had been an agent or, if you like, a valet of a camel merchant. This was not a very illustrious beginning, yet he became a very great man. Let's come back to Jesus, who had nothing in common with him and for whom I continue to have a deep respect, independent even of my religion, which I won't talk about here.

Chapter 32

Research on Jesus

Bolingbroke, Toland, Woolston, Gordon, and other Free-thinkers have concluded from what was written in favor of Jesus and against his person that he was a fanatic who wanted to make a name for himself among the people of Galilee.

The *Toledot Yeshu* says that he was followed by two thousand armed men when Judas went to arrest him on behalf of the San-hedrin and that there was a lot of bloodshed. But if this is true, it is evident that Jesus was as much a criminal as Bar Kochba who called himself the Messiah afterward. It would follow that his conduct answered to some points of his doctrine, "I am come not to bring peace but the sword." What could also make us speculate that Judas was an officer of the Sanhedrin, sent to disperse the ringleaders of Jesus' party, is that the Gospel of Nicodemus, accepted for four centuries and cited by Tertullian and Eusebius, acknowledged as authentic by the emperor Theodosius, this Gospel, I say, begins by introducing Judas among the chief magistrates of Jerusalem who went to accuse Jesus before the Roman praetor. These magistrates were Annas, Caiphas, Summas, Datham, Gamaliel, Levi, Alexander, Nephtalim, and Karoh.

We see by this agreement between the friends and enemies of Jesus that he was in fact pursued and taken by someone named Judas. But neither the *Toledot* nor the book of Nicodemus says that Judas was a disciple of Jesus and that he betrayed his master.

The *Toledot* and the Gospels are also in agreement about the matter of the miracles. The *Toledot* says that Jesus performed them in his capacity as a wizard. The Gospels assure us that he did them in his capacity as a man sent from God. In fact, in that age and before and after, the universe believed in prodigies. There was no writer who didn't tell of prodigies; and no doubt the greatest that Jesus did in a province subject to the Romans was that the Romans never heard about them. To judge only with reason, we must put aside every miracle, every divination. It is only a question here of examining historically whether Jesus was in fact the head of a faction or only had some disciples. Since we do not have the documents of the trial before Pilate, it is not easy to judge.

If you want to weigh the probabilities, it seems likely by the Gospels that he used some violence and was followed by some hot-headed disciples.

Jesus, if we believe the Gospels, barely arrived in Jerusalem when he chased and mistreated some merchants who were legally authorized to sell pigeons in the forecourt of the temple to those who wanted to sacrifice them. This act that seems so ridiculous to Lord Bolingbroke, Woolston, and all the Freethinkers would be as reprehensible as if a fanatic intruded among us to whip the booksellers who were selling the Book of Common Prayer around St. Paul's. But it is also rather difficult to believe that the merchants established by the magistrates let themselves be beaten and chased by a vagabond stranger just arrived from his town into the capital, unless he had a lot of people following him.

They also tell us that he drowned two thousand pigs. If by this he ruined many families who sought justice, we must agree that according to ordinary laws he deserved punishment. But as the Gospel tells us that Jesus had sent the devil into the bodies of these pigs, in a country that never had pigs, a man who is neither Christian nor Jewish can reasonably doubt this. He will say to the theologians, "Pardon me if in wanting to justify Jesus I am forced to refute your books. The Gospels accuse him of beating innocent merchants, of drowning two thousand pigs, of drying up a fig tree that didn't belong to him and of depriving the owner of it only because this tree didn't

108 GOD AND HUMAN BEINGS

bear figs when *it was not the time for figs*. They accuse him of changing water into wine for guests who *were already drunk*; of being transfigured during the night to speak with Elijah and Moses, of being carried away by the devil three times. I want to make this Jesus just and wise. He wouldn't be either if everything you say were true: and these adventures cannot be true because they aren't appropriate for God or man. In order to appraise Jesus, allow me to cross out the passages of your Gospels that dishonor him. I'll defend Jesus against you.

"If it's true as you say and as is very likely that he called the Pharisees and the teachers of law a brood of vipers, whitewashed tombs, rogues, egomaniacs—names that the priests of all times have sometimes deserved—it was a very dangerous recklessness that more than once cost truly careless people their lives. But you can be a very honest man and say that the priests are rogues."

Therefore, just by consulting simple reason we conclude that we have no monument worthy of faith that shows us that Jesus deserved the punishment by which he died; nothing proves that he was a wicked man.

The time of his punishment is unknown. The rabbis differ from the Christians by fifty years. Irenaeus differs from our common opinion by twenty years. There is a difference of twenty years between Luke and Matthew who, moreover, both draw a genealogy that is absolutely different and absolutely foreign to the person of Jesus. No Roman or Greek writer speaks about Jesus; all the Jewish evangelists contradict each other about Jesus; finally, as we know, neither Josephus nor Philo deign to name Jesus.

We find no document among the Romans that they crucified him. We must, then, pending faith, limit ourselves to this conclusion: there was a lowly Jew from the dregs of society named Jesus, crucified as a blasphemer in the time of the emperor Tiberias, though we cannot know in what year.

Chapter 33

On the Morality of Jesus

It is very probable that Jesus preached good morals in the towns, seeing that he had disciples. A man who plays the prophet can say and do crazy things for which he only deserves to be locked up: our Millenarians, Pietists, Methodists, Mennonites, Quakers said and did outrageous things. The prophets of France came to us and claimed to resurrect the dead.

The Jewish prophets were the craziest of all men in the eyes of reason. Jeremiah put a saddlebag on his back and straps around his neck. Ezekiel (4:12; Hosea 1) ate excrement on his bread. Hosea claimed that God ordered him by special privilege to take a prostitute and then an adulterous woman and have children. This last trait is not edifying; it is even very punishable. But finally, there was never on earth a so-called man sent from God who gathered other men together to tell them, "Live without reason and without law; abandon yourselves to drunkenness and be adulterers, sodomites; pick pockets, steal, murder on the highways and do not forget to murder whomever you have robbed in order that they not accuse you; kill even the suckling babies; it is thus that David dealt with the subjects of the petty king Achish; partner up with other thieves and then stab them in the back instead of sharing the booty with them; kill your fathers and mothers to inherit from them sooner. . . ."

Many men, especially Jews, have committed abominations, but no man preached them in countries even slightly civilized. It is true that the Jews, as an excuse for their robberies, attributed atrocious orders to their Moses. But at least they adopted the Ten Commandments common to all people. They forbade murder, theft, and adultery; they advised children to obey their fathers and mothers, just like all ancient lawmakers. To succeed, you always have to encourage virtue. Jesus could preach only an honest morality: there are not two. Epictetus, Seneca, Cicero, Lucretius, Plato, Epicurus, Orpheus, Thoth, Zoroaster, Brahma, Confucius—theirs are absolutely the same.

A crowd of Freethinkers answers us that Jesus departed too far from this universal morality. If you believe the Gospels, they say, he stated that you had to hate your father and mother; that he came into the world to bring a sword and not peace in order to set division among families. His "Make them enter" (Luke 14:25) is the destruction of every society and the symbol of tyranny. He speaks only of throwing in prison the servants who have not put their master's money to work by usury; he wants you to consider anyone who is not part of his church a tax collector. These inflexible philosophers finally find in the books called Gospels as many hateful maxims as base and ridiculous comparisons.

Let us reply to their assertions. Are we so sure that Jesus said what they made him say? Is it very likely (judging only with common sense) that Jesus said he would destroy the temple and rebuild it in three days; that he conversed with Elijah and Moses on the mountain; that he was carried away three times by the "Knat-bull," the devil—the first time in the desert, the second on the roof of the temple, the third on the hill from which he could see all the kingdoms of the earth— and that he argued with the devil?

Furthermore, do we know what meaning he attached to words that (supposing he really said them) can be explained in a hundred different ways, seeing that they were parables, enigmas? It is impossible that he ordered anyone not belonging to his church to be considered a tax collector because at the time he didn't have a church.

But take the sentences that they attribute to him and that are the least susceptible to an ambiguous interpretation, and we see the love of God and neighbor, the universal morality.

As far as his actions, we can judge them only by what they report to us. And do we see even one (besides the affair of the merchants in the temple) that betokens a meddling, seditious disturber of the public order, such as is depicted in the *Toledot Yeshu*?

He went to weddings, consorted with extortionists and prostitutes; it was not to conspire against the powers that be. He did not encourage his disciples to defend him when the law came to take him away. Woolston will say, as much as he wants, that when Simon Barjone cut off the ear of the sergeant Malchus and Jesus gave his ear back, this is one of the most impertinent stories that idiotic fanaticism could have made up. He proves at least that the author, whoever he was, considered Jesus a peaceful man. In brief, the more you consider his conduct (such as they report) with simple reason, the more this reason will convince you that he was an honest enthusiast and a good man who had the weakness of wanting to be spoken about and who did not like the priests of his time.

We can make this judgment only by what was written about him. In the end, his panegyrists portray him as a just man. His adversaries impute to him no other crime but to have stirred up two thousand men; and this accusation is found only in a book full of inanities. In all likelihood, then, he was not at all harmful and he did not deserve his punishment.

The Freethinkers insist, they say, that since he was given the punishment of thieves he must have at least been guilty of some attack against the public tranquility.

But only consider what crowd of good men the outraged priests have killed. It is not only those who came up against the rage of priests who were persecuted by them in every country except in ancient Rome, but the cowardly magistrates borrowed the hands and voice of priestly vengeance from Priscillian up to the martyrdom of the six hundred sacrificed under our infamous Mary; and they continued these legal sacrifices among our neighbors. What tortures and murders! Were not scaffolds and gallows erected throughout Europe for whoever was accused by priests? What! We'll take pity on Jan Hus, Jerome of Prague, the archbishop Cranmer, du Bourg, Servetus, and so forth, and we won't take pity on Jesus?

"Why take pity on him?" they ask. He established a bloody sect that has spilled more blood than the cruelest wars of men ever shed.

No. I dare to put forth, along with the most educated and wisest of men, that Jesus never dreamt of founding this sect. Christianity, such as it was at the time of Constantine, was farther from Jesus than from Zoroaster or Brahma. Jesus became the pretext of our fanatical doctrines, of our persecutions, of our religious crimes, but he wasn't the author of them. Many have considered Jesus a Jewish doctor whom foreign quacks made the head of their pharmacy. These quacks wanted to make people believe that they had taken their poisons from him. I would like to think that I can prove that Jesus was not a Christian, that on the contrary he would have condemned with horror our Christianity such as Rome has made it, an absurd and barbaric Christianity that debases the soul and makes the body die of hunger until the day when both will burn together for eternity. Christianity that, in order to enrich the monks and those people no better than them, has reduced people to begging and, consequently, to the necessity of crime; Christianity that exposes kings to the first devout assassin who wants to sacrifice them for the holy church; Christianity that robs Europe to hoard in the house of the Madonna of Lorette, transported from Jerusalem to Ancona in the air, more treasures than could feed the poor in twenty kingdoms; Christianity, finally, that could have given comfort to the earth but covered it with blood, carnage, and all kinds of innumerable misfortunes.

Chapter 34

On the Religion of Jesus

Since it was reported in all the Gospels, isn't there the strongest evidence that Jesus was born of a Jewish mother and father, that he was circumcised as a Jew, that he was baptized as a Jew in the Jordan with the baptism of justice by the Jew John; like a Jew, that he went to the Jewish temple, that he followed all the Jewish rites, that he observed the Sabbath and all the Jewish holidays and, finally, that he died a Jew?

I will say more; all his disciples were surely Jews. None of those who wrote the Gospels dared to say that Jesus Christ wanted to abolish the law of Moses. On the contrary, they made him say, "I am come not to destroy the law, but to fulfill it." He said elsewhere, "Don't they have the law and the prophets?" Not only do I challenge you to find a single passage where it was said that Jesus renounced the religion in which he was born, but I challenge you to be able to distort, to corrupt a single one whereby you could reasonably infer that he wanted to establish a new worship upon the ruins of Judaism.

Read the Acts of the Apostles. Bolingbroke, Collins, Toland, and a thousand others say that this book is stuffed with lies, ridiculous miracles, clumsy stories, anachronisms, and contradictions, like all the other Jewish books of old. I agree for the moment. But it is for this very reason that I am putting this forward. If in the book where they dared to report so many falsities, according to you, the author of Acts never dared to say that Jesus had instituted a new religion, if the author of this book was never so bold as to say that Jesus was God, mustn't we agree that our Christianity today is absolutely opposed to the religion of Jesus and is even blasphemous?

Let us transport ourselves to the day of the Pentecost when the spirit (whatever this spirit may be) descended upon the heads of the apostles in tongues of fire in a loft. Think only about the speech that the author of the Acts gave to Peter, a speech that they consider the first profession of faith of the Christians. You tell me it's gibberish, but beneath the gibberish you will see traces of truth.

First Peter cites the prophet Joel who said, "I will pour out my spirit on all flesh" (2:17). Peter concludes from this that in their capacity as good Jews he and his companions received the spirit. Notice carefully his words: "You know that Jesus of Nazareth was a man whom God made famous by the powers and prodigies that God did through him" (2:22). Notice above all the value of the words "a man whom God made famous"; this is a very authentic avowal that Jesus never pushed blasphemy to the point of calling himself a real participant in divinity and that his disciples were far from imagining this blasphemy.

"God resurrected him, arresting the pains of hell . . ." (2:24). So it is God who resurrected a man. "It is Jesus whom God resurrected and afterward he was raised up by the power of God . . ." (2:32–33). Notice that in all these passages Jesus was a good Jew, a just man whom God protected, whom he let suffer the death penalty publicly for the truth, but whom he resurrected secretly.

"At the same time Peter and John went up to the temple for the prayer of the ninth hour" (3:1). This irrefutably proves that the apostles persisted in the Jewish religion as Jesus had done. "Moses said to our fathers, the Lord your God will raise up among your brothers a prophet like me; listen to everything he tells you. . . . Whoever does not listen to this prophet will be cut off from among his people" (3:22–23). I admit that Peter, to whom they give this speech, reported very badly the words of Deuteronomy attributed to Moses. Nowhere does the text of Deuteronomy say, "Whoever does not listen to this prophet will be cut off from among his people."

I also admit that there are more than thirty texts of the Old Testament that were falsified in the New Testament to make them fit with what they said of Jesus; but even this falsification is a proof that the disciples of Jesus considered him only a Jewish prophet. It is true that they sometimes called Jesus "Son of God," and we are not ignorant of the fact that "Son of God" means "just man" and "Son of Belial" means "unjust man." The scholars say that they used this ambiguity to attribute divinity to Jesus Christ later on. To tell the truth, they take the name "Son of God" literally in the Gospel attributed to John. It is also said that the expression in this sense was considered blasphemous by the high priest.

When Stephen spoke to the people before being stoned, he said to them, "Was there ever a prophet whom your fathers did not persecute? You killed all who preached the coming of the Righteous One, whom you betrayed and murdered" (7:52). Stephen only gave to Jesus the name of "Righteous One"; he was very careful not to call him God. When Stephen was dying, he did not renounce the Judaic religion; no apostle renounced it. They only baptized in the name of Jesus like they baptized in the name of John the baptism of justice.

Paul himself, who started out being the servant of Gamaliel and ended up being his enemy; Paul whom the Jews claimed had a falling out with Gamaliel because the priest refused him his daughter in marriage; Paul who, after he had been a henchman of Gamaliel and persecuted the disciples of Jesus, of his own accord joined the ranks of the apostles; Paul who was so enthusiastic and so carried away, considered Jesus Christ a man—he was far from calling him God. He did not say in any place that Jesus had not submitted to the Jewish law; Paul himself was always a Jew. "I have not sinned," he said to the proconsul Festus, "against the Jewish law or against the temple" (Acts 25:8). Paul himself went to sacrifice in the temple for seven days: Paul circumcised Timothy, son of a pagan and a prostitute.

"The true Jew," he said in his Epistle to the Romans, "is he who is Jewish on the inside" (2:28–29). In short, Paul was never anything but a Jew who joined the ranks of the partisans of Jesus against the other Jews. In all the passages where he speaks about Jesus Christ, he always extols him as a good Jew with whom God communicated, whom God exalted, whom God set in his glory. It is true that Paul sometimes placed Jesus immediately above the angels and sometimes below. What can we conclude from this? That the unintelligible Paul was a Jew who contradicted himself.

It is very certain that the first disciples of Jesus were nothing but a particular sect of Jews, like the Wycliffists were only a particular sect among us. Jesus certainly must have been loved by his disciples because a few years after his death those who embraced his party wrote fifty-four Gospels, some of which have been preserved entire, others were known by long fragments and some cited only by the church fathers. But neither in the citations nor in the fragments nor in any of the Gospels entirely preserved was the character of Jesus ever proclaimed except in his capacity as a just man upon whom God spread his greatest graces.

Only in the Gospel of John, which is probably the latest Gospel of all, obviously falsified since then, do we find passages concerning the divinity of Jesus. It declares in the first chapter that he is the Word, and it is clear that this first chapter was composed in later times by a Platonic Christian. The term *Word*, "Logos," was absolutely unknown to all the Jews.

However, this Gospel of John made Jesus positively say, "I rise up to my father who is your father, to my God who is your God" (20:17). This passage contradicts all the passages that might make us consider Jesus a God-man. Every Gospel is contradictory to itself and to the others. And all, they say, were falsified or corrupted by copyists.

They falsified much more an Epistle attributed to this same John. They made him say, "that there are three who testify in heaven, the Father, the Word, and the Holy Spirit; and these three are one. And there are three who testify on earth, the spirit, the water, and the blood; and these three are one" (1 John 5:7–8).

It has been proven that this passage was added to the Epistle of John around the sixth century. I will talk in another chapter about the enormous falsifications that the Christians were not ashamed of making and that they call "pious frauds." Here I want only to uncover the truth of everything that concerns the character of Jesus and show clearly that he and his first disciples were always consistently part of the Jewish religion. Let me say in passing that it is proven by this that it is as absurd as it is abominable for the Christians to burn the Jews, who are their fathers. For, when the Jews were sent to the pyre, they should have said to their infernal judges, "Monsters, we have the religion of your God, we do everything your God did. *And you burn us!*"

Chapter 35

On the Manners of Jesus, the Establishment of the Sect of Jesus, and Christianity

The greatest enemies of Jesus have to agree that he had the rare quality of attracting disciples. You do not acquire this domination over minds without some talents, without some manners free of shameful vices. You have to make yourself respectable to those whom you want to lead; it is impossible to make people believe you when they despise you. Whatever they wrote about him, he had to have had diligence, strength, gentleness, temperance, the art of pleasing, and, above all, good manners. I would dare call him a rustic Socrates: both preached morality, both without any apparent mission, both with disciples and enemies, both insulted priests, both were tortured and deified. Socrates died calmly; Jesus is depicted by his disciples as fearing death. Some writer with hollow ideas and contradictory paradoxes, while insulting Christianity, dared to say that Jesus "died as God." Did he see gods die? Do gods die? I don't think this author of so much rubbish ever wrote anything more absurd; and our ingenious Walpole was right to have written that he despised him.

It does not appear that Jesus was married, although all his disciples were, and among the Jews it was a kind of disgrace not to be. Most of those who aspired to be prophets lived without wives, either because they wanted to distance themselves from ordinary customs in everything or because they were embracing a profession that always exposed them to hatred, persecution, and even death and, always being poor, they rarely found a wife who dared to share their miseries and danger.

Neither John the Baptist nor Jesus had a wife, at least that is what we believe; they devoted themselves entirely to their profession, and since they were tortured to death like most other prophets, they left behind them disciples. In this way Zadok formed the Sadducees. Hillel was the father of the Pharisees. They claim that someone named Judas was the principle founder of the Essenes at the time of the Maccabees; the Rechabites, even more austere than the Essenes, were the oldest of all.

The disciples of John were established around the Euphrates and in Arabia; they are still there. They are those who are corruptly called the Christians of St. John. The Acts of the Apostles (19:1–5) says that Paul met many in Ephesus. He asked them who had conferred upon them the Holy Spirit. "'We've never heard of your Holy Spirit,' they answered. 'But what baptism have you received?' 'John's.'" Paul assured them that Jesus' was better. They couldn't have been persuaded, because today they only consider Jesus a simple disciple of John.

Their antiquity and the difference between them and the Christians are quite noticeable in the formula of their baptism; it is entirely Jewish. Here it is: "In the name of the ancient powerful God who is before the light and who knows what we do."

The disciples of Jesus remained for some time in Judea, but being chased away they withdrew into the cities of Asia Minor and Syria where there were Jews. Alexandria and even Rome were full of Jewish brokers. The disciples of Paul, Peter, and Barnabas went to Alexandria and Rome.

Up to now no trace of any new religion. The sectarians of Jesus were content to say to the Jews, "You crucified our master who was a good man. God resurrected him. Ask forgiveness of God. We are Jews like you, circumcised like you, faithful like you to the Mosaic Law; we don't eat pork, black pudding, or hare because they ruminate and have not a cloven hoof (although they don't have a cloven hoof and don't ruminate), but we will loathe you until you confess that Jesus is better than you and you live with us as brothers."

Thus hatred divides the Jews who are enemies of Jesus and his sectarians. In the end they take the name of Christians. Christian means follower of a Christ, of an anointed one, of a Messiah. Soon schism broke out among them without the Roman Empire being in the least aware of it. Men from the vilest rabble fought among themselves over quarrels unknown to the rest of the world.

Entirely separated from the Jews, how could the Christians, then, be said to belong to the religion of Jesus? No more circumcision except at Jerusalem; no more Judaic ceremonies—they no longer observed the rites that Jesus had observed. It was an utterly new cult.

The Christians of different cities wrote their Gospels that they carefully hid from the other Jews, the Romans, and the Greeks; these books were their secret mysteries. But what kind of mysteries, say the Freethinkers. A heap of prodigies and contradictions; the absurdities of Matthew are not those of John, and those of John are different from Luke's. Each little Christian society had its grimoire that it showed only to its initiates. It was a horrible crime among the Christians to let their books be seen by others. This was so true that no Roman or Greek writer among the pagans for four whole centuries ever spoke about the Gospels. The Christian sect very strictly forbade its initiates to show their books, even more so to hand them over to those whom they called profane. Whoever of their brothers talked about them to these infidels was made to suffer long penance.

The schism of the Donatists, as you know, happened in 305 when some bishops, priests, and deacons handed over the Gospels to officers of the empire; they called them "traditors" from which we get the word "traitor." Their colleagues wanted to punish them. They convened the Council of Cirta in which there were the most violent quarrels to the point that a bishop named Purpurius, accused of having murdered two of his sister's children, threatened to make all the bishops his enemies (*Ecclesiastical History*, IX).

We see here that it was impossible for the Roman emperors to abolish the Christian religion because they knew it only at the end of three centuries.

Chapter 36

Innumerable Frauds of the Christians

For three centuries nothing was easier for Christians than to secretly multiply their Gospels until they had fifty-four of them. It is even surprising that there were not more of them. In return, I admit that they were constantly busy with composing fables, imagining false prophecies, false commandments, false adventures, falsifying ancient books, fabricating martyrs and miracles. They called them "pious frauds." There is a prodigious multitude of them. There are the Letters of Pilate to Tiberius and of Tiberius to Pilate, the Letters of Paul to Seneca and of Seneca to Paul, a history of Pilate's wife, Letters of Jesus to a so-called king of Edessa, some edict of Tiberius to put Jesus in the rank of the gods, five or six apocalypses like dreams of a delirious man, a Testament of the twelve patriarchs who preached Jesus Christ and the twelve apostles, the Testament of Moses, the Testament of Enoch and of Joseph, the Ascension of Moses into Heaven, that of Abraham, Elda, Moda, Elijah, Sophonius, and so on, the Voyage of Peter, the Apocalypse of Peter, the Acts of Peter, the Recognitions of Clement, and thousands more.

Above all they imagined apostolic constitutions, decrees in which they did not fail to say that the bishops were superior to the emperors.

They pushed the insolence so far as to imagine Greek verses attributed to the Sibyls that are exceptional in their excess of the ridiculous.

Finally, the four first centuries of Christianity offered only a continual succession of forgers who wrote hardly anything but books of lies. I confess this painfully. It is on these lies that the Christian priests fed their little flocks. They well knew it, Abadie and the other hired writers who tried to justify, if possible, the Christian sects in order to get some petty benefice from the archbishop of Dublin fattened on our substance. They have nothing to say to these terrible accusations, and they have never answered them. And when they were forced to say something, they quickly passed over all these falsifications, over all the counterfeits of the first centuries, over the robbery of councils, over the long collection of deceptions. They acted like the Prussian deserters who passed by the switches to be a little less whipped.

Then they very quickly threw themselves on the prophecies like in a desert covered with thorns and thistles where they thought no one could follow them; they thought they could save themselves in the midst of ambiguities. If a patriarch named Jacob (Gen. 49:11) said that Judah bound his donkey's foal to the vine, they tell you that Jesus entered Jerusalem on a donkey and they claim that the donkey's foal of Judah was a prediction of the donkey of Jesus.

If Isaiah (8:3) said that he had a child with the prophetess his wife and that the child was called Maher-Shalal-Hash-Baz, this meant that Mary of Bethlehem, being a virgin, would give birth to the child Jesus.

If the same Isaiah (53:1–7) lamented that they did not listen to him, if he compared himself to a root in dry land, if he said that he had no respect, that he was considered a leper, that he was beaten down by the iniquities of the people, that he was led to slaughter like a sheep, and so on, all this applied to Jesus.

I read in the *Testament* of the celebrated Meslier that in explaining like this the works of those whom they call the Nabi, the prophets among the Jews, the whole story of Don Quixote was clearly predicted. Let me mention that this parish priest, the most charitable and honest of men, on his deathbed asked forgiveness of God for having accepted an occupation in which he was obliged to deceive men. In his huge *Testament* he recorded the motives of his repentance—it is a known and proven fact—but the opinion of the priest from Picardy is not a proof for an Englishman; I have to have others.

The first are the errors and false citations that are found in the Gospels. St. Luke said (2:1–4) that Quirinius was governor of Syria when Jesus was born. This falsity is known to everyone; we know that the governor was Quintilius Varus. There, they say, is one of the grossest and best-known lies that have ever sullied history. It alone is enough to discredit all the Gospels and prove that they were written only a long time afterward. It is exactly as if one of our pamphleteers wrote that the battle of Blenheim, which signaled the reign of Queen Anne, took place under the reign of George I. I confess that I was devastated by this lie and that the most shameless or the most idiotic commentator, even a Calmet, cannot compensate for it.

Matthew said (2:14–15) that the flight of Jesus into Egypt was predicted by Hosea (11:1), and according to Luke he never went to Egypt. Matthew said that Jesus lived in Nazareth to fulfill the prophecy that assured "that he will be called a Nazarean"; and this prophecy is found nowhere.

Lord Bolingbroke in his *Important Examination* doesn't stop saying that all of it is full of predictions like this or "entirely imaginary or interpreted, like those of Merlin and Nostradamus, with deceitfulness that's disgraceful and absurdity that is pitiful." I am only reporting his words, I am not adopting them; it's up to the reader to judge them.

The tales of miracles are no less foolish, if we believe all the Freethinkers. Jerome wrote in all seriousness that a raven carried a half loaf of bread every day to the hermit Paul in the desert of the Thebaid for forty years, that the raven carried an entire loaf the day that the hermit Anthony came to visit the hermit Paul, and that when Paul died, the following day two lions came to dig a grave with their claws. Saint Pachomius paid his visits riding a crocodile.

The history of martyrs is still more marvelous. The prefect of Rome had the deacon Lawrence cooked on a six-foot-long grill. Saint Potamienne was boiled in pitch for not wanting to sleep with the governor of Alexandria and came out of it with the freshest, whitest skin, which must have inspired new desires in the governor. Seven unmarried Christian women from the city of Ancyre, the youngest of whom was seventy years old, were condemned to be raped by all the young men of the city, or rather the young men were condemned to rape them, and this is the most natural event in their history.

All the Christian miracles were like their martyrs. The most terrible of these miracles was the one reported in the Acts of the Apostles. They said that Ananias and Saphira his wife, two proselytes of St. Peter, suddenly died right after each other because they didn't give all their money to the apostles. They were guilty of hiding some shillings in order to live and of not confessing it to St. Peter. What a miracle, great God, and what apostles!

Most of the miracles were more pleasant. St. Gregory Thaumaturgus, that is, "the wonder-worker," first learned his catechism from the mouth of a lovely old man who came down from heaven. Hardly had he learned his catechism when he wrote a letter to the devil. He placed it on the altar; the letter was dutifully carried to its address; and the devil did not fail to do everything the wonder-worker ordered him to do. The annoyed pagans wanted to seize him and his disciple. They were both immediately changed into trees and escaped the pursuit of their enemies.

You will easily believe that the Christians enlarged the number of their martyrs and their miracles at the same time. What partisan writers have not exaggerated everything that could attract the goodwill of the public to themselves? They exaggerate for the sole pleasure of being read or listened to, all the more reason when fanaticism and the interest of a faction seem to authorize the lie. But the secret archives of the Christians have been lost since the year 300. Pope Gregory I admitted this in his seventh letter to Eulogius. They found nothing left in his time except a very small part of the *Acts of the Martyrs* by Eusebius. Everything they wrote since then on the ancient martyrs and the ancient miracles can therefore only be a collection of fables.

The one clearly proven miracle they show us will be the one that we believe. I have heard of about five or six hundred miracles performed in our time in France on behalf of the convulsionists. The list was given to the king of France by a magistrate who himself witnessed the miracles. What happened to him? The magistrate was locked up like the lunatic he was; they mocked these miracles in Paris and in the rest of Europe.

To certify the miracles, they have to do exactly the opposite than was done in Rome when they canonized a saint. They begin by waiting for the saint to die and then waiting at least one hundred years, after which when the saint's family or even the province involved in his apotheosis has 100,000 ecu ready for the expenses of the Apostolic Chamber, they compare the evidence that they'd heard about fifty years before from old women who knew him to a large extent, testifying that fifty years ago the saint in question had healed their aunt or their cousin of a dreadful headache when saying a mass for their recovery.

It is not like this that one puts the work of God above all suspicion. The best, no doubt, is to go about it like we did in 1707 when Fatio de Duillier and the gentleman Daude came to us from the mountains of Dauphiné and Cevennes with two or three hundred prophets in the name of the Lord. We asked them by what prodigy they wanted to prove their mission. The Holy Spirit declared by their mouths that they were ready to resurrect a dead man. We permitted them to choose the most stinking corpse they could find. This act was played out in the public square in the presence of the superintendents of Queen Anne, the regiment of guards and a huge crowd. The result, as you know, was to put the so-called resurrectors in the pillory. Maybe a hundred years from now some new prophet will find in the archives that the fanatic Fatio and the imbecile Daude really did bring a dead man back to life and that they were pilloried only through the perversity of miscreants, who never give in to the evidence.

The first Christians must have done it like this, which our doctor Middleton very clearly perceived. They must have presented themselves before the full Senate and said, "Conscript Fathers, be kind enough to give us a body to resurrect. We are confident of our deed, even if it's only a dressmaker like Dorcas who darned the dresses of the faithful and whom Saint Peter resurrected; we are ready, command." The Senate would not have failed to put the Christians to the proof. A corpse brought back to life by their prayers or by a sprinkling of holy water would have baptized the whole Senate of Rome, the emperor and the empress; and they would have baptized all the Roman people without the slightest difficulty. Nothing was easier, simpler. This was not done; let them tell us the reason why if they can.

But let them first tell us how the Christian religion finally managed to subjugate the Roman Empire with fables that seem to Bolingbroke, Collins, Toland, Woolston, and Gordon to deserve only horror and scorn. They won't be surprised at this if they read the following chapters. But they must read them in the spirit of a philosopher, a good man who is not yet enlightened.

Chapter 37

On the Causes of the Progress of Christianity, On the End of the World and the Resurrection Announced about Its Time

I have spoken only following the weak principles of reason. I will continue with this honest freedom. Fear and hope on the one hand and the enchanting theology on the other have always held absolute empire over weak minds; and there are weak minds among rulers just like among inn servants.

After the death of Caesar there arose in the Roman Empire a rather common opinion that the world was going to end. The horrible wars of the triumvirs, their proscriptions, the three parties' plundering of the then known land contributed not a little to strengthen this idea among the fanatics.

The disciples of Jesus took advantage of this so well that in one of their Gospels the end of the world was clearly predicted and the epoch was fixed for the end of the generation contemporary with Jesus Christ. Luke (21:25–32) was the first to speak of this prophecy, soon adopted by all the Christians. "There will be signs in the moon and stars, roaring of the sea and streams, men consumed with fear will await what has to happen to the entire universe. The forces of the heavens will be shaken and then they will see the Son of Man coming in a cloud with great power and majesty. Verily I tell you that the present generation will not pass before all this is accomplished."

The enlightened head of Paul more than once frightened his disciples from Thessalonica by stating this prophecy: "We who are living and speaking, we will be carried away before the Lord in the midst of the air."

Simon Barjone, called Peter, whom Jesus, they say, named with a strange ambiguity to be the cornerstone of his church, said in his First Epistle, "The end of the world is approaching" and in his Second, "We are waiting for a new heaven and a new earth." The First Epistle of John affirms that "the world is in its final hour." Thaddeus, Jude, or Judas saw "the Lord who will come with thousands of saints to judge men."

Since this catastrophe did not happen in the generation when it was announced, they postponed it to a second generation and then a third. A New Jerusalem, in fact, appeared in the air for several nights. A few church fathers saw it distinctly, but it disappeared at the break of dawn like devils who flee at the crow of a cock.

So they postponed the new heaven and the new earth to a fourth generation; and from century to century the Christians waited for the end of the world that was so imminent.

To this fear was joined the hope of a kingdom of heaven that the Gospels compared to a mustard seed, to a wedding banquet, to money put in usury. What was this kingdom? Where was it? Was it in the clouds where they had seen the Jerusalem of the apocalypse? Was it in the seven planets or in a star of the greatest magnitude or in the Milky Way through which our vicar Derham saw the firmament?

Paul had assured the Jews of Thessalonica that he was going with them, body and soul, through the air to this firmament. But another, no less seductive opinion prevailed at the time of Paul and Jesus, which was that they would be resurrected to enter the kingdom of heaven.

Paul tried to tell the Thessalonians that they would go straight to the firmament without dying; they sensed it even though they all gave up the ghost like other men and Paul himself died; but they cajoled themselves with the resurrection.

This hope was not a new idea. Metempsychosis was a kind of resurrection. The Egyptians embalmed their bodies only so that they might get their souls back one day. Resurrection is clearly proclaimed in the *Aeneid* (6.713–15): "Souls, to which by fate are owed another body, at the shores of the river Lethe drink the untroubled waters and long oblivion."

They were already arguing about this resurrection in Jerusalem at the time of Jesus. The thing is hardly possible in the eyes of a reasoning, learned man, but it is a comfort to an ignorant man who hopes and doesn't reason. Firstly he imagines that the faculty of thinking and feeling will go straight to paradise where it will think and feel without organs. Then he figures that when his organs have become dust scattered to the four corners of the earth, they will reshape into their first form in a million centuries, cross all the heavenly globes, and that he will be the same man as he once was; and that having thought and felt for so many centuries without a body, he will finally think and feel with his body, which he really has no need of but that he loves forever.

Plato was not an enemy of resurrection; he resurrected Er for fifteen days in his *Republic*. I don't know for sure how long Lazarus was resurrected. My fellow countrymen who travel in the southern parts of France can easily find out: for Lazarus went to Marseilles with Mary Magdalene and the monks of this area no doubt have his death certificate.

Some dreamer named Bonnet, in a collection of jokes he called *Palingenesis*, seems convinced that our bodies will be resurrected without stomachs and without parts in front and behind, but with "intellectual fibers" and excellent heads. Bonnet's seems to me a little cracked; we should put it with Ditton's. When he is resurrected, I advise him to ask for a little more common sense and for fibers that are a little more intellectual than he was given while alive. But whether Charles Bonnet is resurrected or not, Lord Bolingbroke, who has not yet been resurrected, proved to us during his life how much all these chimeras entice idiots bewitched by fanatics.

It is useful that men believe God is a rewarder and revenger. This idea encourages honesty and is not shocking to common sense; but resurrection is offensive to all thinking people and even more so to those who calculate. It is a very bad policy to want to govern men with fictions. For, sooner or later their eyes will be opened and they will hate the errors on which they have been fed, all the more so for having been enslaved by them.

In the beginning the people blindly surrendered to half-Jews, half-Christians, half-Platonists who had the eagerness to make proselytes, eagerness so dear to pride. The ignorant and the disciples of the ignorant attracted others to their side; and the women, always very devoted and credulous, were made Christians by the same weakness that others were made witches.

This was undoubtedly not enough for the Roman senators, the successors to Scipio, Cato, Metellus, Cicero, Varro, to become infatuated with such a "tale of a tub." And in fact there was hardly any senator before Theodosus who embraced such a chimerical sect. Constantine himself, when the Christians' money made him emperor and he openly gave credit to this party that had become the richest, had to leave Rome forever, where the senators hated him, and establish Christianity in his new city of Constantinople.

So, for Christianity to triumph to such an extent, he had to use more powerful means than this fear of the end of the world, this hope for a new earth and new heaven, and this desire to live in a new, heavenly Jerusalem.

Platonism was the strange force that gave it consistency and activity when it was applied to the budding sect. Rome did not enter into this mix of Platonism and Christianity for nothing. The secret bishops in Rome during the first centuries were only very ignorant half-Jews who knew only how to pile up money, but of philosophical theology they knew nothing. We find no bishop of Rome among the church fathers for six entire centuries. It was in Alexandria, which had become the center of sciences, that the Christians became reasoning theologians, and this alleviates the baseness that we criticize them for in their origin; they became Platonists in the school of Alexandria.

Certainly no honorable man, no thinking man would have joined their faction if they were not satisfied saying, "Jesus was born of a virgin; the ancestors of his putative father trace back to David by two entirely different genealogies. When he was born in a stable three wise men or three kings came from the heart of the East to worship him in his trough. King Herod, who died then, didn't doubt that Jesus was a king who would dethrone him one day and he had the throats of all the children in the neighboring towns cut, figuring that Jesus would be caught up in the massacre. His parents, according to the evangelists, who cannot lie, took him to Egypt; and according to others, who also cannot lie, he stayed in Judea. His first miracle was to be carried away by the devil onto a mountain from where he could see all the kingdoms of the earth. His second miracle was to change water into wine at a wedding of peasants when they were already drunk. By his omnipotence he dried up a fig tree that didn't belong to him because he found no fruit on it at a time when it wasn't supposed to bear any, for it wasn't the season for figs. He sent the devil into the body of two thousand pigs and made them die in the middle of a lake in a country where there were no pigs . . . , and when he had performed all these lovely miracles, he was hanged."

If the first Christians had said only this, they would have attracted no one to their party, but they wrapped themselves in the doctrine of Plato and then some half-reasonable men took them for philosophers.

Chapter 38
Platonic Christians—the Trinity

All the metaphysicians, all the theologians of antiquity were necessarily charlatans who could not be understood. The words alone point this out. Metaphysics: "above nature." Theology: "knowledge of God." How can we know what is not natural? How can man know what God thought and what he is? The metaphysicians had to use only words because the physicians used only them and they had to dare to reason without experience. Metaphysics until Locke was only a vast field of chimeras; Locke was truly useful only because he narrowed the field where they wandered. He was right and made himself understood only because he was the only one who understood himself.

The obscure Plato, more talkative than eloquent, more a poet than a philosopher, sublime because we barely understand him, became admired among the Greeks, Romans, Asians, and Africans by his dazzling sophisms. When the Ptolemies established their schools in Alexandria, they were Platonists.

In a bombastic style Plato had spoken of a god who formed the world with his word. Sometimes this word was the Son of God, sometimes it was the Wisdom of God, sometimes it was the world that was the Son of God. In truth there is no Holy Spirit in Plato, but there is a kind of Trinity. This Trinity, if you like, is power, wisdom, and bounty. If you also like, it is God, the word, and the world. If you like, you will even find it in these lovely words of one of the letters to his capricious and vicious friend Dionysius the Tyrant: "The most beautiful things have their first cause in God, their second in perfection have their second cause in him, and he is the third cause of works of the third degree."

Aren't you satisfied with this Trinity? Here is another in his *Timaeus*: "It is the indivisible substance, the divisible, and the third that takes after both."

All this is really marvelous; but if you love Trinities, you will find them everywhere. You will see Isis, Osiris, and Horus in Egypt; in Greece Jupiter, Neptune, and Pluto, who share the world between them; Birma, Brahma, and Vishnu are the Trinity of the Indians. Three has always been an awesome number.

In addition to these Trinities, Plato had his intelligible world. This was composed of archetypal ideas that always stayed deep in the brain and are never seen.

His great proof of the immortality of the soul in his dialogue of Phaedo and Echecrates was that "the living come from the dead and the dead from the living." And from this he concludes that "souls after death go into the kingdom of Hades." All this lovely nonsense earned Plato the title "divine," just like the Italians today give it to the charming fool Ariosto who is, however, more intelligible than Plato.

What there is in Plato of the divine or somewhat profound fanaticism that approaches madness they studied in the school of Alexandria for more than three hundred years. All this metaphysics is even much older than Plato; he got it from Timaeus of Locri. We see a strong descent of romantic ideas among the Greeks. The Logos is in Timaeus. And Timaeus had taken it from Orpheus. In Clement of Alexandria and in Justin you can find this fragment of a hymn of Orpheus, "I swear by the word that proceeds from the father and that became his counselor when he created the world."

This doctrine was finally given so much authority by the Platonists that it got through into the Jews of Alexandria. Philo, born in this city and one of the most learned Jews and a very honest Jew, was a zealous Platonist. He even went farther than Plato because he said that God "was married to the word and the world was born of this marriage." He called the word God.

So the first followers of Jesus who came to Alexandria found Platonic Jews there. It must be mentioned that there were at that time
many more Jews in Egypt than you could imagine in the time of the
pharaohs. They even had a very beautiful temple in Bubastis,
although their laws forbade them to sacrifice anywhere but in
Jerusalem. All these Jews spoke Greek, and that is why the Gospels
were written in Greek. The Greek Jews were hated by those in
Jerusalem, who cursed them for having translated their Bible and who
atoned for this sacrilege every year with a gloomy festival.

So it was not difficult for the followers of Jesus to attract some of
their brothers from Alexandria and other cities who hated the Jews of
Judea. They were joined above all by those who had embraced the
doctrine of Plato. This was the great core and the first development of
Christianity. This was the real beginning of this religion. There was a
public school of Platonic Christianity in Alexandria, a chair where
Mark taught. (This is not the one whose name is at the head of a
Gospel.) Mark was succeeded by Athenagoras and then Pantaenus;
Pantaenus was succeeded by Clement, called the Alexandrine; and
Clement by Origen, and so forth.

This was where the word was made known to the Christians; this
was where Jesus was called "the Word." The whole life of Jesus
became an allegory and the Jewish Bible was no more than another
allegory that predicted Jesus. In time the Christians had a Trinity;
everything became mystery to them; the less it was understood, the
more importance it got.

Among the Christians there was not yet a question of three distinct substances composing one single God and named the Father,
Son, and Holy Spirit. They fashioned the Gospel of John and stitched
onto it a first chapter in which Jesus was called "Word" and "light of
light"; but not a word about the Trinity such as they have confessed
since then, not a word about the Holy Spirit considered God.

This Gospel told about those who listened to Jesus, "They had not
yet received the spirit, the spirit blows where it wants," which only
means the wind. It said that Jesus "was troubled in his spirit," which
means he died; "having said this, he blew on them and told them,
Receive the spirit." Now, it doesn't seem that they sent God into the
bodies of people by blowing on them. This was, however, a very
ancient method: the soul was a breath, and all the so-called magicians

blew and blew again upon those on whom they imagined they were casting a spell. They made an evil spirit enter into the mouths of those whom they wanted to harm. An evil spirit was a breath; a beneficent spirit was a breath. Whoever invented these silly things certainly did not have much of a mind, in whatever sense you take this rather vague and uncertain word.

Could they ever have foreseen that they would one day make of this word—breath, wind, spirit—a supreme being, a God, the third person of God, proceeding from the Father, proceeding from the Son, having no paternity, not made nor engendered? What appalling "non-sense"!

A great objection to this nascent sect was: "If your Jesus is the word of God, how did God allow them to hang his word?" They answered this striking question with even more incomprehensible mysteries. Jesus was the Word, but he was a second Adam. Now, the first Adam had sinned, so the second had to be punished. It was a very great offense against God: for Adam had wanted to be wise and to become so he had eaten an apple. Since God is infinite he was infinitely annoyed; so he needed an infinite satisfaction. The Word, in its capacity as God, was also infinite; so it alone could satisfy. It was hanged not only as Word, but also as man. So it had two natures; and from the wondrous combination of these two there resulted even more wondrous mysteries.

This sublime theology astonished the minds and did no wrong to anyone. Whether or not the half-Jews worshipped the Word, the world went its normal way; nothing was disturbed. The Roman Senate respected the Platonists, it admired the Stoics, it loved the Epicureans, it tolerated the remains of the religion of Isis. To the Jews it sold the freedom to build synagogues in the middle of Rome. Why would it have persecuted Christians? Made people die for saying that Jesus was a word?

The Roman government was the most gentle on earth. We have already remarked that no one had been persecuted for thinking.

Chapter 39

On Christian Dogma Absolutely Different from That of Jesus

Properly speaking neither the Jews nor Jesus had any dogma. Do what is commanded by the law. If you have leprosy, show yourself to the priests; they are excellent doctors. If you have a bowel movement, do not forget to carry a steel-tipped staff and cover up your excrement. Do not move on the day of the Sabbath. If you are suspicious of your wife, make her drink the waters of jealousy. In the month of Nisan eat a roast lamb with lettuce, having shoes on your feet, a staff in your hand, a belt around your waist, and eat quickly, and so on.

This is not dogma, not theological discussions. These are observances to which we see that Jesus was always subject. We do nothing that he did, and he proclaimed nothing that we believe. He never said in our Gospels, "I have come and I will die to take away the original sin. My mother is a virgin. I am consubstantial with God and there are three of us persons in God. As to myself I have two natures and two wills and I am only one person. I do not have paternity and yet I am the same thing as God the Father. I am he and I am not he. The third person will one day proceed from the Father according to the Greeks and from the Father and Son according to the Latins; the whole universe was born condemned and my mother as well: nevertheless, my mother is the mother of God. I command you to put my entire body, my hair, my nails, my beard, my urine, my blood in a little piece of bread by speaking and at the same time, separately, to put all my blood in a chalice of wine. So that they drink the wine and eat the bread and yet they are destroyed. Remember that there are seven virtues, four cardinal and three theological, that there are only seven capital sins, like there are only seven sorrows, seven beatitudes, seven heavens, seven angels before God, seven sacraments, which are visible signs of invisible things; and seven kinds of grace, which correspond to the seven branches of the candelabra."

What am I saying? Did we ever learn what our soul is; if it is a substance or a faculty narrowed to a point or spread out in the body preexisting in our body or when it entered it? He gave us so little notion of this that many church fathers wrote that the soul is corporeal.

Jesus spoke so little about dogma that every Christian society that arose after him had its own belief. The first who reasoned were called Gnostics, that is to say "knowing," who were divided into Barbelonites, Florians, Phebeonites, Zachaeans, Codices, Borborites, Ophites, and many other little sects. Thus the Christian Church never existed for a single moment united; it is not today; it never will be. Unity is impossible unless the Christians are wise enough to sacrifice their invented dogma for morality. But isn't it also impossible for them to become wise? All we can guarantee is that there are many who will become so and even who already do become so every day, despite the barbaric hypocrites who constantly want to put theology in place of virtue.

Chapter 40

On Christian Disputes

Discord was the cradle of the Christian religion and will probably be its grave. From the time since Christians have existed, they have insulted the Jews, their fathers, insulted the Romans under the empire where they lived and insulted one another in turn. Hardly did they preach Christ before they accused one another of being the anti-Christ.

More than six hundred disputes, great and small, raised and maintained trouble in the Christian Church while all the other religions of the earth were at peace; and what is more true is that there is not one of these theological disputes that was not based on absurdity and fraud. Look at the war of tongues, pens, swords, and daggers between the Arians and the Athanasians. It was all about knowing if Jesus was like the Creator or if he was identified with the Creator. Both of these propositions were equally absurd and impious. You will certainly not find it stated in any of the Gospels. The partisans of Arius and those of Athanasius battled "for the shadow of the soul." The emperor Constantine, in whom the crimes had not extinguished common sense, began by writing to them that they were all fools and that they were dishonoring themselves by such frivolous and impertinent quarrels. This is the substance of the letter that he sent to the heads of these two factions, but soon afterward the ridiculous desire to assemble a council, to preside over it with a crown on his head and the vain hope of bringing the theologians into agreement, made him as foolish as they were. He convened the Council of Nicaea to know precisely if a Jew was God. There is the excess of absurdity; there now is the excess of fraud.

I won't speak about the intrigues that the two factions employed, the countless lies and calumnies; I will limit myself to the two lovely miracles that the Athanasians performed at the Council of Nicaea.

One of these miracles that is recorded in the appendix to the Council (Concil. Labb. vol. 1, p. 84) is that the church fathers, being hard-pressed to decide which Gospels, which pious writings it was necessary to adopt and which to reject, decided to put all the books that could be found in a pile on the altar and invoke the Holy Spirit, which, of course, made all the bad books fall on the ground; the good books remained and since that moment there should have been no more doubt.

The second miracle recorded by Nicephorus (book 8, chap. 23), Baronius (vol. 4, n. 82) and Aurelius Peruginus (ann. 325) was that two bishops named Chrysantus and Musonius died while the council was being held and were not able to sign the condemnation of Arius, so they came back to life, signed, and died again. This proves how necessary it is to condemn heretics.

It seemed that they had to wait for a formal decision on the Trinity from this grand council; there was no question about it. They were satisfied saying a short word at the end in the profession of faith of the council. The fathers afterward declared that Jesus was engendered and not made and that he was consubstantial with the Father; they declared that they also believed in the breath that we call the Holy Spirit and of which we have since made a third God. It must be admitted with a modern author that the Holy Spirit was treated very offhandedly at Nicaea. But what is this Holy Spirit? We find in the twentieth chapter of John that when Jesus was secretly resurrected, he appeared to his disciples, breathed on them and said, "Receive my holy breath." And today this breath is God.

The Council of Ephesus, which anathematized Nestorius, the patriarch of Constantinople, is no less curious than the First Council of Nicaea. After having declared Jesus God, they did not know in what rank to put his mother. Jesus dealt with her harshly at the wedding in Cana; he said to her, "Woman, what is there between you and me?" and he flatly refused at first to change water into wine for the young men at the wedding. This affront had to be repaired. St. Cyrillus, bishop of Alexandria, resolved to make Mary acknowledged as the mother of God. It seemed a bold undertaking at first. Nestorius, patriarch of Constantinople, vigorously declared from the pulpit that it was making Mary seem too much like Cybele, that it was surely right to give her honors, but was a little too much to give her suddenly the rank of mother of God.

Cyrillus was great at talking nonsense. Nestorius too. Cyrillus was a persecutor; Nestorius less so. Cyrillus made many enemies because of his unruliness; Nestorius made even more; and the fathers of the Council of Ephesus in 431 were given the pleasure of deposing them both. But though these two bishops lost their case, the Holy Virgin won hers: she was finally declared the mother of God and everybody clapped their hands.

Afterward they proposed to admit her into the Trinity, which seemed only right because as she was the mother of God, they could not refuse her the quality of goddess. But since the Trinity would have then become a quaternity, it seems that the arithmeticians opposed it. They could have responded that since three made one, they could also make four; or that four could make one if they liked. These fine quarrels still go on and there are many Nestorians today who are brokers of change among the Turks and Persians, like the Jews are among us. Beautiful catastrophe of a religion!

Jesus spoke about his two natures and his two wills no more than about the divinity of his mother. He never let it be suspected while he was alive that he had only one person in him with two wills and two natures. They held councils to shed light on these systems and it was not without a very great upheaval in the empire.

Never did Jesus have any image in his house, unless it was the portrait of his mother that they say was painted by St. Luke. They may repeat that he had no house, that he knew not where to lay his head, that though he were as well housed as our Archbishop of Canterbury, he knew no worship of images; they may thoroughly prove that for three centuries the Christians had no statues, no portraits in their gatherings. Nevertheless, a Second Council of Nicaea declared that they had to worship images.

We know well enough what quarrels we had about transubstantiation and about so many other points. "Finally," the Freethinkers say, "take the Gospel in one hand and your dogma in the other, see if there is any of this dogma in the Gospel; and then judge whether the Christians who worship Jesus belong to the religion of Jesus. Judge whether the Christian sect is not a bastard Jewish sect, born in Syria, raised in Egypt, chased in time from the place of its birth and its cradle, presently ruling over modern Rome and other Western countries with money, fraud, and executioners." Let us not hide the fact that this is the discourse of the most educated men of Europe and let us confess before God that we need universal reform.

Chapter 41

On the Customs of Jesus and the Church

By the customs and manners I understand here the conduct, the harshness or gentleness, ambition or moderation, greed or selflessness. All you have to do is open your eyes and ears to be certain that in all these things there has always been more difference between the Christian churches and Jesus than between the storm and the calm, between fire and water, between day and night.

Let's speak a moment about the pope in Rome, even though we have not recognized him in England for almost two and a half centuries. Is it not evident that a fakir from India is more like Jesus than a pope? Jesus was poor, went from town to town to serve his neighbor, led a wandering life; he went on foot, never knew where he would sleep, rarely where he would eat. This is exactly the life of a fakir, a talapoin, a santon, a marabout. The pope in Rome, on the other hand, is housed in Rome in the palace of emperors. He has around 800,000–900,000 pounds sterling in revenue when his finances are well managed. He is humbly an absolute sovereign, he is a servant of servants, and in this capacity he has deposed kings and conferred almost all the kingdoms of Christianity; he even has a king as vassal to the shame of the throne.

Let's move on from the popes to the bishops. They have all imitated the pope as much as possible. They have everywhere appropriated royal rights; they are sovereigns in Germany and among our barons of the kingdom. No bishop truly takes the title of servant of servants; on the contrary, almost all Papist bishops are entitled bishops by permission of the servant of servants, but all are allocated sovereign power. There is not found one among them who did not want to crush secular authority and magistracy. They themselves are the ones who tell the popes to dethrone kings; the bishops of France deposed Louis, son of Charlemagne, long before Gregory VII was insolent enough to depose the emperor Henry IV.

Spanish bishops deposed their king Henry IV the Impotent; they claimed that a man in this state was not worthy of reigning. The name of Henry IV had to be very unlucky since Henry IV of France, who was very worthy of reigning for the opposite reason, was nevertheless declared incapable of the throne by three-fourths of the bishops of the kingdom, by the Sorbonne, and by the monks as well as the popes.

These detestable mummeries are today considered with as much contempt as horror by all nations, but they were revered for more than two centuries and Christians were treated like beasts of burden by the bishops everywhere. Still even today in the unfortunate Papist countries, the bishops despotically meddle in individuals' business. They make them eat what they want at certain times of the year; what's more, they suspend at their whim the cultivation of the land. They order the feeders of the human race not to work, not sow, not harvest on certain days of the year and on some occasions they push their tyranny so far as to forbid them to obey Providence and nature for three days in a row. They condemn people to criminal idleness by their private authority, without the people daring to complain, without the magistrates daring to make use of the power of civil laws, the only reasonable power.

If the bishops have usurped the rights of princes everywhere, we must not believe that the pastors of our reformed churches have had less ambition and fury. We have only to read in our historian philosopher Hume about the somber and absurd atrocities of our Presbyterians in Scotland. The blood boils at such a reading; one is tempted to punish, for the insolences of their predecessors, those who today spread the same principles. Every priest, I have no doubt, would be, if he could, a tyrant of the human race. Jesus was only a victim. See, then, how they resemble Jesus!

If they answered me what I heard many of them say, that Jesus communicated to them a right that he did not deign to use, I would repeat what I told them that in this case it is up to the Pilates of our day to make them suffer the punishment that their master did not deserve.

We burned two Arians under the reign of James I. What were they guilty of? Not to have attributed to Jesus the epithet of consubstantial that he surely did not give himself. The son of James I bore his father's head on a scaffold; our infamous religious disputes were the principal cause of this patricide. He was no guiltier than the two Arians executed under his father.

Chapter 42

On Jesus and the Murders Committed in His Name

We have to take Jesus Christ as they give him to us. We can only judge his customs by the conduct that they attribute to him. We do not have a Clarendon or Hume who wrote his life. His evangelists imputed to him no other action of a violent and hotheaded man than to have very inopportunely beaten and chased away the merchants of sacrificial animals who had their store at the entrance of the temple. Except for this, he was a very gentle man who hit no one, and he resembled our Quakers who do not like to spill blood. You even see how he put back the ear of Malchus when the very unstable and weak St. Peter had cut off the ear "of that constable" a few hours before denying his master. Do not tell me that this affair is the height of the ridiculous; I know it as well as you. But I am also obliged again to judge here only on the evidence that has been presented in the case.

Therefore, I suppose that Jesus was always honest, gentle, and modest. Let's examine a little how the Christians have imitated these words and what good their religion has done for the human race.

It will not be inopportune to make here a short list of all the men whom it has massacred either in seditions or battles or on the scaffold or at the stake or by murders that are holy, premeditated, or suddenly inspired by the spirit.

The Christians had already stirred up some trouble in Rome when in 251 of our common era the priest Novatian disputed what we call the See of Rome, the papacy, with the priest Cornelius: for it was already an important place that was worth a lot of money. And exactly at the same time the See of Carthage was also disputed by Cyprian and another priest named Novatus who had killed his wife by kicking her in the stomach (*Eccles. Hist.*). These two schisms caused many murders in Carthage and Rome. The emperor Decius was forced to suppress this madness with some punishment, which we call the great, the terrible persecution of Decius. I won't speak about that here; I will limit myself to the murders of Christians committed by other Christians. When we count only two hundred people killed or seriously wounded in these two first schisms that were the model of so many others, I think that this list won't be too large. So, let's put down:

200

When the Christians could surrender themselves with impunity to their holy vengeance under Constantine, they murdered the young Candidianus, the son of the emperor Galerius, the hope of the empire, whom they compared to Marcellus; an eight-year-old child, son of the emperor Maximinus; a seven-year-old daughter of the same emperor; their mother the empress was dragged out of the palace with her servants into the streets of Antioch and they were all thrown into the Orontes. The empress Valeria, widow of Galerius, and the daughter of Diocletian were killed in Thessalonica in 315 and had the sea for a tomb.

It is true that some writers did not accuse the Christians of this murder and imputed it to Licinius; but let's cut the number of those whose throats the Christians cut on this occasion to two hundred. That's not too much. Here:

200

In the schism of the Donatists in Africa, we can hardly count fewer than four hundred people bludgeoned by clubs because the bishops did not want to fight with swords. Put:

400

You know what horrors and how many civil wars the single word *consubstantial* was the origin of and pretext for. This blaze lit up the whole empire and was rekindled in all the provinces devastated by the Goths, Burgundians, and Vandals for almost four hundred years. When we only put three hundred thousand Christians slaughtered by Christians in this dispute without counting the roving families reduced to begging, you cannot reproach me for padding the accounts. Here:

300,000

The dispute of iconoclasts and icon worshippers certainly did not cost less than sixty thousand lives:

60,000

We should pass over in silence the one hundred thousand Manichaeans whom the empress Theodora, widow of Theophilus, had killed in the Greek Empire in 845. It was a penance that her confessor had ordered because up to that time they had hanged, impaled, and drowned only twenty thousand. All these people well deserved to be killed for teaching that there was only a good principle and a bad principle. The total rises to one hundred and twenty thousand at least. Here:

120,000

We will count only twenty thousand in the frequent seditions incited by priests who quarreled everywhere over Episcopal sees. We must use extreme discretion. Put:

20,000

They calculated that the horrible madness of the Holy Crusades cost the lives of two million Christians. But I would like to reduce it by the most astonishing reduction to one million. Here:

1,000,000

The crusade of the Livonian Brothers of the Sword, who devastated all the shores of the Baltic Sea with such honesty and sanctity, should count at least one hundred thousand dead. Here:

100,000

The same goes for the crusade against Languedoc, where for a long time we saw only pyres and bones of the dead devoured by wolves in the country. Here:

100,000

For the crusades against the emperors since Gregory VII, I would like to count only fifty thousand. Here:

50,000

The Great Schism of the West in the fourteenth century killed enough people to justify our moderation, if we count only fifty thousand victims of the papal rage, *rabbia papale*, as the Italians say. Here:

50,000

The devotion with which they burned the two priests Jan Hus and Jerome of Prague in the city of Konstanz at the end of the Great Schism brought much honor to the emperor Sigismund and the council, but it caused, I know not how, the Hussite War in which we can confidently count one hundred and fifty thousand dead. Here:

150,000

After these great butcheries, I admit that the massacres at Mérindol and Cabrières are a slight thing. It was only a matter of twenty-two large towns set on fire, eighteen thousand innocents slaughtered and burned, suckling babies thrown in the flames, girls raped and quartered, old women who were no longer good for anything and whom they made jump into the air by sticking powder cartridges in their two orifices. But since this small execution was done lawfully, with all the formalities of justice, by men in robes, this party of the French right must not be left out. Put here:

18,000

Now we come to the holiest, the most glorious epoch of Christianity, which some vagabonds wanted to reform at the beginning of the sixteenth century. The holy popes, the holy bishops, the holy abbots refused to be modified, so the two parties marched on the bodies of the dead for two entire centuries with only a few intervals of peace.

If the reader would like to take the pain of putting together all the murders committed from the reign of Pope Leo X to that of the holy Pope Clement IX, either lawful or unlawful murders; heads of priests, of seculars; princes slaughtered by the executioner; the price of wood increased in many provinces because of the multitude of pyres lit up, blood spilled from one end of Europe to the other; the executioners grown weary in Flanders, Germany, Holland, France, England; thirty civil wars for transubstantiation, predestination, the surplice and holy water; the massacres of St. Bartholomew, the massacres of Ireland, Vaudois, Cévennes, and so forth, you would no doubt find more than three million unfortunate families plunged in a misery worse, perhaps, than death. But since it is only about the dead here, let us quickly pass over this horror, two million. Here:

2,000,000

Let us not be unjust; let us not ascribe more crimes to the Inquisition than it committed in surplice and stole; let us not exaggerate anything. Let's reduce the number of souls that it sent to heaven or hell to two hundred thousand. Here:

200,000

Let's even reduce to five million the twelve million men that the Bishop Las Casas claimed to have sacrificed for the Christian religion in America and, above all, make the comforting remark that they were not men seeing that they were not Christians. Here:

5,000,000

Let us reduce with the same economy the four hundred thousand men who perished in the civil war of Japan incited by the reverend Jesuit fathers; let's bring the count just to three hundred thousand. Here:

300,000

———————

Total: *9,468,800*

The total calculation will only rise to the sum of 9,468,800 people, either with their throats cut or drowned or burned or mauled or hanged for the love of God. Some half-learned fanatics will answer me that there was a frightening multitude of Christians dying by the most horrible torments under the Roman emperors before Constantine; but I would say to them with Origen, "There were very few persecutions and only from time to time." I would add, "When you have as many martyrs as the Golden Legend of dom Ruinart the Benedictine laid out, what will that prove? That you were always intolerant and cruel; that you forced the Roman government, the most humane of the world, which gave total freedom to the Jews and Egyptians, to persecute you; that your intolerance served only to spill your blood and shed the blood of other men, your brothers and that you are guilty not only of murders, with which you covered the earth, but also of your own blood, which you once shed. You have made yourselves the most unhappy of all men because you were the most unjust."

Whoever you may be, reader, if you preserve the archives of your family, consult them and you will see that you had more than one ancestor sacrificed on the pretext of religion or at least cruelly persecuted (or persecuting, which is even more grievous); if you are called Argyle, Perth, Montrose, Hamilton, or Douglas, remember that they tore out the hearts of your fathers on the scaffold for the sake of a liturgy and two ells of cloth. Are you Irish? Just read the declaration of the English parliament of July 25, 1643: it said that in the Irish conspiracy 154,000 Protestants perished at the hands of Catholics. Believe, if you want, with the lawyer Brooke, that there were only forty thousand men defenselessly slaughtered in the first movement of this holy and Catholic conspiracy. Whatever the calculation, you descend from murderers or murderesses. Choose and tremble. But you, prelate of my country, rejoice—your blood has earned you five thousand guineas' rent.

My calculation is frightening, I admit, but it is far below the truth. I know that if they presented this calculation to a prince, a bishop, a canon, a tax collector while they dining with their masters and singing lewd songs, they would not deign to read it. The devotees of Vienna, Madrid, Versailles will not even take the trouble to examine if the calculation is right. If by chance they learn about these astonishing truths, their confessors will tell them that they must recognize the hand of God in all these butcheries, that God could do no less on behalf of a small number of elect; that since Jesus suffered the death penalty, all Christians, from whatever sect they may be, should die likewise; that it is a horrible impiety to not kill right away all the little children who come to receive baptism because then they will be eternally happy through the merits of Jesus and that letting them live they risk damning them. I feel the force of all these arguments, but I am going to propose another system with the defiance that our own lights of reason should provide to us.

Chapter 43

Honest Propositions

Our dean Swift wrote a great book in which he believed to have proven that it was not yet time to abolish the Christian religion. I am of the same opinion: it is a tree that, as the whole earth admits, has borne only the fruits of death; nevertheless, we don't want to just cut it down, we want to graft it.

I propose keeping in the morality of Jesus everything that conforms to universal reason, to that of all the great philosophers of antiquity, of all times and all places, to that which should be the eternal bond of all societies.

Let us worship the Supreme Being through Jesus, since it is established thus among us. The five letters that compose his name are certainly not a crime. What does it matter if we render our homage to the Supreme Being through Confucius, Marcus Aurelius, Jesus, or some other, provided that we are just? Religion surely consists in virtue and not in the impertinent frivolities of theology. Morality comes from God; it is uniform everywhere. Theology comes from men; it is different and ridiculous everywhere. This has been said often before and it must always be said again.

Impertinence and absurdity cannot be a religion. The adoration of a God who punishes and rewards unites all men; the detestable and contemptible argumentative theology divides them.

This argumentative theology is at the same time the most absurd and the most abominable scourge that ever afflicted the earth. The ancient nations were satisfied worshipping gods and did not argue, but we others for centuries have spilled the blood of our brothers for sophisms. Alas! What does it matter to God and to men whether Jesus was Homoousios or Homoiousios, whether his mother was Theotokos or Jesustokos, and whether the spirit proceeds or not? Great God! Was it necessary to hate, persecute, and cut one another's throats for these incomprehensible chimeras! Banish the theologians, and the universe is calm (at least with respect to religion). Accept them, give them authority, and the land is flooded with blood. Aren't we already unhappy enough without making religion, which should comfort us, be used for our miseries? The horrible calamities with which the Christian religion has flooded all the countries it reached for such a long time afflicts me and makes me weep, but the infernal horrors it has spread in the three kingdoms of which I am a member rends my guts. I scorn an icy heart that is not seized by the same transports as mine when it considers the religious troubles that have shaken up England, Scotland, and Ireland. In the times that saw the birth of that too easy, too uncertain King Charles I and that strange Cromwell, half-mad, half-hero, half-fanatic, half-rogue, half-politician, and half-barbarian, Christianity lit the flames that put our cities to ash and furbished the swords that for so long covered our countryside with the corpses of our ancestors.

Unhappy and detestable compatriots, what was the principal cause of your frenzies? You slaughtered each other to know if you needed a surplice or a cassock, for a covenant, for ridiculous, or at least useless, ceremonies.

The Scots sold the king who took refuge with them for 200,000 pounds sterling to the English, the king who was condemned in Rome because he did not submit to the Papist superstition, the king condemned in Edinburgh because he did not submit to the ridiculous Scottish Covenant, the king dead in London on the scaffold because he was not Presbyterian.

Our Irish compatriots carried their frenzy further when, a little before this abominable execution, our Papists murdered a tremendous number of Protestants, when many fed on the flesh of their victims and were illuminated by the candles made from their fat.

What should be noticed by attentive eyes, but with eyes long wet with tears, is that in all these times when Christians were sullied by the religious murders in England, Ireland, Scotland, in the times of Charles I, Charles II, James II, in France from Charles IX to Louis XIII, in Germany, in Spain, in Flanders, in Holland under Charles V and Philip II, in these times, I say, so horrible and close to us, in the mutual massacres committed in the five valleys of Savoy and in the Cévennes in France, all these crimes were justified by the examples of Phinehas, Ehud, Jael, Judith, and all the murderers with whom the Holy Scriptures abound.

There, Christian religion, are your results! You were born in a corner of Syria from which you were chased away, you crossed the seas to come to bear your inconceivable rage to the ends of the continent, and yet I offer to preserve you provided that we trim your nails with which you tore apart my fatherland and your teeth with which you devoured our fathers.

Once again let us worship God through Jesus if we must, if ignorance has prevailed so much that this Jewish word has to be pronounced, but that it not be a word on the lookout for rapine and carnage.

God of innumerable worlds! God of justice and peace, let us atone by our tolerance for the crimes that the detestable frenzy of intolerance made us commit.

Come to me, reasonable Socinian, dear Quaker; come, good Anabaptist, hard Lutheran, somber Presbyterian, indifferent Episcopal (note that we call someone from the sect of bishops Episcopal, someone of the High Church, whereas in France this word is only an adjective, the episcopal grandeur, the episcopal pride), Mennonite, Millenarian, Methodist, Pietist, yourself an insane Papist slave, come, provided that you have no dagger in your pocket; bow down together before the Supreme Being, thank him for having given you fat, young chickens, venison, and good bread for your food, a mind to know them and a heart to love them; dine together merrily after having given him thanks.

Let the Papist princes do what they want with the idol of their pope whom they are all beginning to mock. Let them try with all their might to prevent religion from being a danger in their states. Let them change, if they can, the useless monks into good workers.

Let them not be so stupid anymore as to ask permission of a priest to eat chicken on Fridays. Let them change the schools of theology into hospitals. Let them do all the good they are capable of; it is their business. Ours is to be inviolably attached to our happy constitution; to love God, truth, and our country; and to address our prayers for all men to God the father of all men.

Chapter 44

How We Should Pray to God

I hear the outcry of our clerics; they scream at us, "If it is necessary to worship God in spirit and in truth, if men are wise, there will no longer be public worship, they will no longer come to our sermons, we will lose our benefices." Don't worry, my friends, about the greatest of your fears. We are not rejecting priests, even though in Carolina and Pennsylvania every father of a family can be minister of the Most High. Not only will we keep your benefices, but we also hope to increase the income of those who work the most and who are paid the least.

Far from abolishing public worship, we want to make it purer and less unworthy of the Supreme Being. You feel how indecent it is to sing to God only Jewish songs and how shameful it is not to have been smart enough to make more suitable hymns yourselves. Let us praise God, let us thank God, let us invoke God in the way of Orpheus, Pindar, Horace, Dryden, Pope, and not in the Hebrew way. Sincerely, if you begin today to institute public prayers, who among you would dare to suggest singing the barbaric nonsense attributed to the Jew David?

Aren't you embarrassed to say to God: "You will rule all the nations that you will submit to us with an iron scourge, you will break them like a potter does a vase" (Ps. 2:9)?

"You will break the teeth of sinners" (Ps. 3:7).

"The earth trembled, the foundations of the mountains shook because the Lord was angry at mountains; he cast hail and coals" (Ps. 18:9, 14).

"He lived in the sun and came out like a husband who gets out of his bed" (Ps. 19:5).

"God will break the teeth in their mouth, he will crush their molars, they will become nothing, like water: for, he has drawn his bow to shoot them down and they will all be swallowed up alive in his anger before understanding that your thorns are as tall as a plum tree" (Ps. 58:6–7, 9).

"The nations will come toward evening hungry like dogs and you, Lord, will mock them and reduce them to nothing" (Ps. 59:8–9).

"The mountain of the Lord is a coagulated mountain, why do you look at coagulated mountains? The Lord said, I will cast out Bashan, I will cast it into the sea so that your foot be tainted with blood and the tongues of your dogs lick their blood" (Ps. 68:15–16, 22–23).

"Open your mouth wide and I will fill it up" (Ps. 81:10).

"Make the nations like a wheel that always turns, like straw before the wind, like a fire that burns a forest, like a flame that burns mountains; pursue them with your tempest and your anger will trouble them" (Ps. 83:12–15).

"The Lord will register in the writings of the peoples and princes those who were born in Zion" (Ps. 87:6).

"And my horn will be like the horn of the unicorn [which doesn't exist] and my old age in the mercy of the breast" (Ps. 92:10).

"Your youth will be renewed like the youth of the eagle" [which is not renewed] (Ps. 103:5).

"He will judge the nations, he will fill them with destruction, he will break the head of many rulers in the land" (Ps. 110:6).

"Jerusalem is built like a city whose participation is in itself" (Ps.122:3).

"Blessed is he who will take his children and crush them against a rock" (Ps. 137:9).

You'll admit that the Ode of Horace, "*Coelo tonantem crededimus Jovem*" (Ode 3.5), and one of the secular games are a little more valuable than this dreadful "non-sense" of the old "ballads" (meaning songs) plundered from a people whom you scorn. I pray you to consider to whom they attribute most of these songs. He was a villain who began by being the pet of the little king Saul, became his son-in-law, and revolted against him. He made himself chief of four hundred thieves who plundered, slaughtered women and suckling babies, spent their lives in murder, adultery, debauchery, and who even murdered through his testament. Such was David, such was the man after God's own heart. Our worthy fellow citizen Hewett had no problem calling him a "monster." Great God, can't they praise you without repeating these so-called odes of such a criminal Jew?

Moreover, my dear compatriots, sing little; for, you sing very badly. Pray, but rarely in order to pray better. Too many sermons demean the preaching of the preacher.

As there are necessarily among you many people who have neither the gift of speech nor the gift of thought, they must get rid of the stupid pride of spouting bad speeches and stop boring Christians. They must read to people the beautiful speeches of Tillotson, Smalridge, and others; there are very few of them. Addison and Steele have already advised you of this.

It is a very good institution to gather together once a month or even, if you like, once a week to listen to an exhortation to virtue. But let a moral speech never be an absurd metaphysics, even less a satire, and even less a seditious rant.

God preserve us from banishing public worship. They dared to accuse us of this; it is an atrocious imposture. We want a pure worship. We began two and a half centuries ago to clean out the temples that had become the stables of Augeas; we removed the spider webs, the rotten rags, the bones of the dead that Rome had sent to us to infect the nations. Let's complete such a noble task.

Yes, we want a religion, but a simple one, wise, august, less unworthy of God and made more for us; in a word, we want to serve "God and human beings."

Axioms

No society can survive without justice. Therefore, let us proclaim a just God.

*   *   *

If the state's law punishes known crimes, let us then proclaim a God who punishes the unknown crimes.

*   *   *

Let a philosopher be a Spinozist if he wants. But let the man of the state be a theist.

*   *   *

You do not even know what God is, how he will punish, how he will reward, but you do know that he should be sovereign reason, sovereign equity; this is enough. No mortal has the right to contradict you, since you are saying something probable and necessary to the human race.

*   *   *

If you deface this comforting and terrible probability with absurd fables, you will be guilty against human nature.

*   *   *

Do not say that it is necessary to deceive men in the name of God; this would be devils' talk, if there were devils.

*   *   *

Whoever dares to say, "God spoke to me," is a criminal against God and human beings. For, would God, the common father of all, communicate to only one?

*   *   *

If God wanted to give some command, he would make it understood to the whole earth, like he gave the light to all eyes. Also, his law is in the hearts of all reasonable beings and nowhere else.

*   *   *

It is utterly horrible and ridiculous to proclaim that God is like a crazy, little, barbaric despot who secretly dictates an incomprehensible law to some of his favorites and slaughters the rest of the nation for not having known the law.

*   *   *

God walks! God talks! God writes on a little mountain! God fights! God becomes man! God-man suffers the death penalty! Ideas worthy of *Punch*.

*   *   *

A man predicts the future! Idea worthy of Nostradamus.

*   *   *

To invent all these things is the utmost villainy. To believe them is the utmost stupidity. To put a powerful and just God in place of these astonishing farces is the utmost wisdom.

*   *   *

"But if my people reason, they will rise up against me!" You are mistaken: less if they are fanatical, more if they are faithful.

*   *   *

Barbaric princes say to barbaric priests, "Fool my people so that I might be better served and I will pay you well." The priests bewitch the people and dethrone the princes.

*   *   *

Calchas forces Agamemnon to sacrifice his daughter for wind; Gregory VII makes Henry V revolt against the emperor Henry IV his father, who dies in misery and to whom they refused a grave. Gregory is much more terrible than Calchas.

*   *   *

Do you want your nation to be powerful and peaceful? Let the law of the state rule over religion.

*   *   *

What is the least harmful religion of all? That in which we see less dogma and more virtue. What is the best? It is the simplest.

*   *   *

Papists, Lutherans, Calvinists, they are so many bloody factions. The Papists are slaves who fought under the insignia of the tyrant pope. The Lutherans fought for their princes, the Calvinists for popular liberty.

*   *   *

The Jansenists and Molinists put on a farce in France. The Lutherans and Calvinists staged bloody tragedies to England, Germany, and Holland.

*   *   *

Dogma made ten million Christians die in torment. Morality did not make a scratch.

*   *   *

Dogma also brought division, hatred, and atrocity into the provinces, cities, and families. O virtue, comfort us!

Addendum of the Translator [by Voltaire]

After the chapter on Platonic Christians, I would add one to uphold the opinion of the author, if I were allowed to mix my ideas with his. I could say that all the opinions of the first Christians were taken from Plato, even up to the dogma of the immortality of the soul that the ancient Jews never knew. I would show that the "kingdom of heaven," which is so often talked about in the Gospels, is found in the *Phaedo* of Plato. Here are the very words of the Greek philosopher who, without knowing it, founded Christianity: "Another, pure world is above this pure sky where the stars are; the earth that we inhabit is only the crude sediment of this ethereal world," and so forth.

Plato then adds, "we will see the kingdom of the heavens, the resting place of the blessed, if we can cast ourselves beyond our crude air like fish can see our land when soaring above the surface of the water."

Later here is how it is described: "All is perfect in this perfect land; it produces precious stones to which ours do not compare. . . . It is covered in gold and silver; this sight is the pleasure of the blessed. The weather is always mild; their organs, intelligence and health put them infinitely above us," and so on.

Who doesn't recognize the celestial Jerusalem in this description?

The only difference is that there is at least some philosophy in the celestial city of Plato and there isn't any in that of the apocalypse attributed to St. John. "It is," he says, "like a stone of japser, like a crystal. . . . He who spoke with me had a golden cane to measure the city. . . . The city was built like a square, as long as it was wide, and it was twelve thousand stadia and its length, width, and height were are equal. . . . The first layer of the foundation of the city was jasper, the second was sapphire, the third chalcedony, that is to say agate, the fourth emerald," and so on.

Purgatory, especially, was clearly taken from the *Phaedo*; the words of Plato are remarkable: "Those who are neither entirely criminal not entirely innocent are carried to Acheron and there they suffer punishment proportional to their faults until they have been purged of their sins and then they receive the reward of their good deeds among the blessed."

The doctrine of the Resurrection is also wholly Platonic, seeing that in the tenth book of the *Republic* the Greek philosopher introduces Er resurrected and relating what happened in the other world.

It doesn't much matter whether Plato drew his opinions—or, if you wish, fables—from the ancient Egyptian philosophers or from Timaeus of Locri or from the depths of himself. What is very important to consider is that they were comforting to human nature and this is what made Cicero say that he would rather be wrong with Plato than right with Epicurus. It is certain that bad morality and bad health have taken hold of our short life and that it would be sweet to hope for an eternal life that no evil would dare approach. But why begin by evil to come to good? Why wasn't this eternal and happy life given to us at first? Wouldn't it be ridiculous and barbaric to build for your children a magnificent palace full of all imaginable delights but whose entrance was a dungeon inhabited by toads and snakes and to imprison your children in this horrible dungeon for seventy or eighty years to make them better appreciate afterward all the pleasures with which the palace abounds; pleasures that they will only feel when the snakes in the entrance have devoured their flesh and bones?

Whatever the case may be, it is unquestionable that all this doctrine was spread throughout all of Greece before the Jewish people had the least knowledge of it. The Jewish law that the Jews claim have been given to them by God himself never spoke about the immortality of the soul or the resurrection of the body. It is utterly ridiculous to say that these ideas were implied in the Pentateuch. If they were divine, they should not have been implied—they should have been clearly explained. They did not begin to shine forth to a few Hebrews until long after Plato. Therefore, Plato is the true founder of Christianity.

If you then consider that the doctrine of the Word and the Trinity is explicitly present in no other writer except Plato, it is absolutely necessary to regard him as the sole founder of Christian metaphysics. Jesus, who never wrote anything, who came such a long time after Plato and who appeared only among a crude and barbaric people, cannot be the founder of a doctrine that is older than he and that he surely did not know.

Again, Plato is the father of Christianity and the Jewish religion is its mother. Now, what is more unnatural than to beat up one's father and mother? When a man sticks up for Platonism today, a pedant of theology will present an inquiry to have him burned in a public square, if he can, as the pedant of Noyon [Calvin] once had Michael Servetus burned. If a Spanish *Nuevo Christiano* imitates Jesus Christ, if he is circumcised like him, if he observes the Sabbath like him, if he eats the paschal lamb like him with lettuce in the month of March, the officers of the Inquisition will want to burn him in a public square.

It is an equally remarkable and horrible thing that the Christian sect has almost always spilled blood and that the Epicurean sect that denied Providence and the immortality of the soul has almost always been peaceful. Not even a slap has been given in the history of the Epicureans and there is perhaps not one single year from Athanasius and Arius up to Quesnel and Le Tellier that hasn't been marked by exiles, imprisonments, thievery, murders, conspiracies, or mortal combat.

Plato undoubtedly did not imagine that one day his sublime and unintelligible reveries would become the pretext of so many abominations. If they have so horribly perverted philosophy, the time has come at last to return it to its former purity.

All the ancient sects except the Christians supported one another, so let us support even the Christians; but also let them support us. Let them not be an intolerant monster: just because the first chapter of the Gospel attributed to John was evidently composed by a Christian is not a reason to persecute me. Let the priest who is fed, clothed, and housed with the tithes that I pay him, who survives only by the sweat of my brow or that of my tenants, no longer claim to be my master, and a vicious master; I pay him to teach morality, to set an example of gentleness, and not to be a tyrant.

Every priest is in this situation; the pope himself has officers, valets, and guards only at the expense of those who cultivate the land and who are born his equals. There is no one who does not feel that the power of the pope is founded solely on prejudices. Let him no longer abuse it; let him fear lest these prejudices vanish.

Biblical Citations Index

Old Testament citations are in order according to the Roman Catholic Canon

Name and Subject Index

Shalmaneser, 62

Shaphan, 69

Shasta, 27

Shreve, Michael, 9–10

Silenus, ass of, 96

Simon Barjone, 28, 111, 126
    See also Peter, Saint (the Apostle)

Sinai, 45, 53, 54

Sisera, 65

Sixtus IV (pope), 21

Smallridge, 155

Socrates, 47, 117

Solomon (king), 21, 38, 59, 62, 63, 67,
    99, 100
    existence of, 80

Solon, 75

Song of Solomon. *See* Canticle of
    Canticles

"Son of God," 133
    meaning of, 115, 130

soul, 30–31, 46–47, 135
    immortality of, 30, 43, 46–47, 71,
        161
        Chinese not admitting to, 37,
            43
        and double doctrine, 47–49
        Epicureans not believing in,
            47–48
        not found in Pentateuch,
            162–63
        not present in Jewish law,
            71–73
        and Plato, 131
        Roman philosophers denying,
            71

Spinoza, Baruch, 157

state vs. religion, 159

Steele, Richard, 155

Stephen, Saint, 60, 115

Strabo, 82

stupidities of mankind, 17–19, 25

remedies for, 20–21

superstitious beliefs, 48

widows burning selves, 31

Summas, 106

Supreme Being, 22
    how to pray to, 153–55
    as seen by the Arabs, 30
    as seen by the Brahmin, 27, 30
    as seen by the Chinese, 25
    as seen by the Greeks, 46
    as seen by the Romans, 50
    worshipping through Jesus, 149,
        151
    See also God

Swift, Jonathan, 149

Sydney, Algernon, 80

Syncellus, George, 93

Syria, religion in, 71

Tacitus, 82

Tamar, 65

Tartarus, 50

Ten Commandments, 78, 110

Tertullian, 106

Testament (Meslier), 121

theism, 157

Theodectes, 54

Theodora (empress), 145

Theodosius (emperor), 106

Theodosus, 128

theology, 13, 27, 43, 47, 125, 130, 163
    argumentative theology, 149–50
    Christian theology, 13, 15, 135.
        See also Christianity
    Jewish theology, 69, 128, 133. *See
        also* Judaism
    See also religion

Theophilus (emperor), 145

Theopompus, 54

Theudas, 101

Thobel [Tubal], 82